THE LAWYER WITHOUT A SUIT

Make More Money, Have More Freedom,
and Never Set Foot in a Courtroom Again

THE
LAWYER
WITHOUT
A SUIT

Make More Money, Have More Freedom,
and Never Set Foot in a Courtroom Again

WILL WORSHAM

Copyright © 2024 by Will Worsham

All rights reserved. No part of this book may be used or reproduced in any manner whatsoever without prior written consent of the author, except as provided by the United States of America copyright law.

Published by Best Seller Publishing®, St. Augustine, FL
Best Seller Publishing® is a registered trademark.
Printed in the United States of America.
ISBN: 978-1-962595-74-2

This publication is designed to provide accurate and authoritative information with regard to the subject matter covered. It is sold with the understanding that the publisher is not engaged in rendering legal, accounting, or other professional advice. If legal advice or other expert assistance is required, the services of a competent professional should be sought. The opinions expressed by the author in this book are not endorsed by Best Seller Publishing® and are the sole responsibility of the author rendering the opinion.

For more information, please write:
Best Seller Publishing®
1775 US-1 #1070
St. Augustine, FL 32084
or call 1 (626) 765-9750
Visit us online at: www.BestSellerPublishing.org

CONTENTS

Foreword..vii

Chapter 1: The High-Tech Hillbilly Lawyer 1

Chapter 2: Burn Your Lawyer Suit and Find the
Freedom Mindset...11

Chapter 3: Change Your Billing and Change Your Life....27

Chapter 4: The Estate Planning Secret............................ 39

Chapter 5: Systems and Scalability.................................49

Chapter 6: Staying Focused on the Clients 59

Chapter 7: Building Your Support Staff 71

Chapter 8: Introduction to Seminars............................... 85

Chapter 9: When Good Seminars Go Bad 95

Chapter 10: The Successful Speech.................................111

Conclusion: Take the Plunge.. 135

Bonus Chapter 1: Working with a Financial Planner........145

Bonus Chapter 2: Working with a Professional Speaker...153

FOREWORD

I first crossed paths with Will Worsham on the bustling set of a local television show, where our shared commitment to excellence quickly became apparent. As we fielded viewer inquiries within our respective domains of expertise, it became evident that Will and I were cut from the same cloth. Both driven by a relentless pursuit of client satisfaction and a fervent desire to innovate, our encounter marked the beginning of a transformative partnership.

With nearly four decades of experience in financial planning under my belt, I had accompanied countless clients on their estate planning journeys, often grappling with the limitations of conventional legal services and the lack of viable alternatives. Despite my conviction that there had to be a better way, the elusive solution remained just out of reach—until Will entered the picture.

In Will, I found a kindred spirit—a visionary entrepreneur armed with a background in technology and a track record of success with MissouriTrafficTickets.com. Together, we bemoaned the deficiencies of existing estate planning paradigms and resolved to chart a new course, one marked by innovation, efficiency, and accessibility.

Over the ensuing months, Will and I embarked on a collaborative journey, dissecting the shortcomings of traditional legal practices and devising pioneering solutions to better serve our respective clienteles. Will's keen insight, honed not only in the intricacies of estate planning but also in practice development, fee structuring, and staff management, proved indispensable in shaping our revolutionary approach.

With a laser focus on cutting through the clutter of conventional wisdom, Will engineered a system that delivered premium-quality services at unprecedented speed and cost efficiency. In doing so, he not only elevated the standard of client care but also forged a thriving solo practice that outpaced larger firms in both revenue and client satisfaction.

Nearly a decade since our fortuitous encounter, I now count Will as both a cherished friend and a trusted advisor. Witnessing his transition from a successful criminal defense attorney and entrepreneur to a trailblazer in the realm of estate planning has been nothing short of inspiring. Yet, amidst Will's remarkable accomplishments, I couldn't help but wonder why more legal professionals hadn't followed suit.

The answer, it seemed, lay in fear—fear of departing from familiar conventions, fear of embracing the unknown, and fear of failure. But as Will's groundbreaking methods demonstrated, knowledge serves as the antidote to fear. With this book, Will not only imparts invaluable insights into the principles and practices of modern estate planning but also emboldens fellow attorneys to confront their apprehensions and seize the boundless opportunities that lie ahead.

In these pages, readers will find not only a roadmap to professional rejuvenation but also a testament to the transformative power of courage, innovation, and unwavering dedication. May Will's wisdom embolden and inspire a new generation of legal professionals to chart their own course toward a brighter future—for themselves, their clients, and the legal profession at large.

Warm regards,

Bruce Porter, IAR, Principal
The Resource Center - Financial Planning & Insurance Services
Springfield, MO

CHAPTER 1

THE HIGH-TECH HILLBILLY LAWYER

It's 2:30 in the afternoon on a hot August Friday in 2015 in southwest Missouri. I've been practicing criminal law for almost twenty years. I sit in the hallway at the Greene County Courthouse, wearing a suit and tie, and I am uncomfortable. Not just in my suit but also in my skin. I'm waiting for the judge to call my case; it was scheduled for 1:15, but what's an extra hour or two of sweltering stagnation?

My client is up for sentencing on a mid-level felony offense to which he'd pled guilty, and this is the last place I want to be today, but for some reason, circuit judges *love* to do felony sentencing on Friday afternoons. This isn't my first rodeo. This isn't even my hundredth rodeo. I know exactly what's going to happen: the prosecutor is going to ask for an outrageously harsh sentence, then I'm going to ask for an unreasonably light sentence. The victims are going to say how horribly their lives have been affected, and my client is going to plead for mercy. Then the judge, well, he's going to do what he's already decided to do and fall somewhere in the middle.

No one is going to be happy. Not the prosecutor, not me, not the victims, not the judge, and certainly not my client. Not a single person will be pleased with the outcome of this sentencing.

Sitting in that hallway, thinking about going through this process, oh, I don't know how many times, I just knew in my heart I didn't want to do it anymore. Odds were this client still owed me money that I knew I was never gonna see. They didn't care that I had secretaries to pay, an office to pay for, utility bills to cover, and needed a salary for myself. The Bar Association wanted their dues, and quite frankly, I felt trapped, knowing that I'd have to agree to represent yet another person in the exact same situation to cover the bills and earn my living. It was then that I realized I was just looking for a way out.

> No one is going to be happy. Not the prosecutor, not me, not the victims, not the judge, and certainly not my client.

Once in the courtroom, things went well for my client—as well as they could—but of course, it wasn't good enough. I don't know if I could have heard, "But O.J. got off..." one more time. Some people are ungrateful, and some are grateful. Once, on the same day that a client screamed at me for getting her three months of unsupervised probation for keeping a SERIOUS speeding ticket off her record, I read a thank-you card from a client in jail on a thirty-day sentence for his third felony DWI. He knew a month in lockup was better than years in prison. But that's the nature of the criminal defense game... you win some, you lose some, and it takes a physical and mental toll. I was done. It was time to go back to my roots.

Growing Up Hillbilly

I am familiar with the images that the word "hillbilly" evokes for people who aren't from where I'm from. And you know what? I'm okay with that. You can think anything you want about us, but I guarantee the truth will surprise you. I grew up hillbilly, and that meant plenty of time outside, and lots of stories. I'm thrilled to still live on the 120-acre "Century Farm" where I was raised, owned by my grandparents and their parents and their parents before them. We had horses to ride, cattle to tend, and the odd pig to feed every now and then. People who have never been around pigs don't know that they stink, they're mean, they can get huge, and they can kill you by accident. But then again, so can the bull that you bottle-fed from a calf and the horse you've ridden for years. Livestock have a funny way like that. You learn to be wary or be trampled. Your choice.

There were places back in the woods to explore, too, especially a little wet-weather stream that had washed the soil away from some granite buried in the side of a holler. It had even, over time, carved out a little sluiceway through the rocks. It was one of the places I enjoyed walking or riding in, just to see how it looked and appreciate the peace. You could find all sorts of things wandering around in the woods—anything from old animal bones to arrowheads and some rusted tools lost or left behind. People would sometimes search for legendary items in the area, one of which was Abner's head.

Let Me Tell You a Story

Now, it seems that Abner (no one knows the rest of his name or if his name was really Abner) had been in Mansfield and was flashing money around in an unwise, ostentatious show of wealth. He then continued his string of bad decisions by announcing that he'd be traveling down to Ava by horseback. For those unfamiliar with our little corner of the Ozarks, that's about a 15-mile trip, and these days it would take you about twenty minutes by car.

So, Abner hopped on his horse, pockets full of money, and headed south to Ava, and I bet you can guess what happened next. Abner never made it to Ava, but his horse did. Foul play being suspected, a search party began and eventually found Abner's body—sans his head. To this day, neither Abner's head nor his wealth has been found, but searching the area is still an occasional pastime and the subject of news reports on a slow day.

My grandmother-in-law would tell stories from when she worked at a local tourist attraction in nearby Branson, MO. Tourists come to Branson from all over the country to see the shows, go to the theme parks, and enjoy the local lakes and wilderness. While working at one of these venues, she said it was not uncommon for someone to ask somewhat shyly, "Excuse me, where are the hillbillies?" or "Where can we go to find the hillbillies?"

And she would just tell them, "Well, here I am!"

I liked that, and I adopted it in my own way. As I travel around to speak to various groups, and people ask about where I'm from, I say, "Have you ever seen *The Beverly Hillbillies*? Well, we were neighbors before they moved."

> "Have you ever seen *The Beverly Hillbillies*? Well, we were neighbors before they moved."

THAT'S THE HILLBILLY SPIRIT

Ozarks hillbillies tend to be cunning. As another local legend tells, a group of counterfeiters was operating at one time from the local big city of Springfield, MO. Apparently, they decided that the heat was getting a little *too* hot from the local constabulary, so they headed out of town to the woods near the Webster and Douglas County line. That was probably a smart move, but smart moves became a little scarce after that. Having set up shop in the wilderness, they began to run their operation. Unfortunately for them, somewhere in the move there was a mix-up, and they accidentally printed up several stacks of $15 bills.

Rather than waste all the effort and ink, one of these big-brain, big-city criminals decided that, surely, they could buffalo the local hillbillies into taking these bogus bills. So, they headed out to the nearest general store, which happened to be in a small town called Smackout. In fact, the town was named for the store itself. It was run by a little old hillbilly woman who had the habit of, when asked for an item that was out of stock, replying, "Nope! We're smack out!" Hence it came to be the name of the town.

So, into this store, run by this woman, came the counterfeiter with his $15 bills. He walked around a bit and settled on the candy bins in the back. Picking out two 15-cent candy sticks, he headed to the counter. The woman promptly rang up his 30-cent purchase and didn't bat an eye when presented with a $15 bill to seal the deal. Instead, she cashed him out and proceeded to hand him back his change—two $7 bills and two 35-cent pieces.

As you can see, the entrepreneurial spirit runs strong in the Ozarks hillbillies.

TAPPING MY INNER ENTREPRENEUR

I went to junior high at the Logan-Rogersville Junior High School, which had just been realigned as a middle school to include sixth grade, along with seventh- and eighth-grade classes. Because the district was being reorganized and hyphenated, we attended school in the building that had previously been the high school. I was in the first sixth-grade class after the realignment, along with students from the Logan and Rogersville elementary schools. For the record, I attended Logan, and my wife attended Rogersville, but those two student bodies came together in the hyphenated district for middle school and high school.

So, there I was, a lowly sixth grader, tossing around in this ancient, and I mean ANCIENT, high-school building with a dank, dark cafeteria in the basement, of all places. It shouldn't have come as a surprise to anyone that the building was condemned the summer after, and consequently, I spent the rest of junior high attending classes in the old Rogersville Elementary School building while they tried to figure out a more permanent solution. To make it even more interesting, they added fifth grade to the mix. What a time to be alive! But I digress. It was there, as a seventh grader in an elementary school with a large pool of potential clientele, that I embarked on one of my first entrepreneurial endeavors.

My grandmother, well, she lived right next to the school, and my mother was a teacher. So, my normal routine, when school was over, was to walk to my grandmother's house and wait for my mother to collect me after she'd finished her day at Logan Elementary School. I'd usually be with my grandmother for about an hour, watching cartoons and having a snack—typical '80s kid after-school stuff. I got into the habit of riding the bicycle I kept at my grandmother's over to the only grocery store in Rogersville to grab ramen noodles or other things I could fix by myself. Sometimes I would get a candy bar, and those cost 35 cents. Thirty-five cents! What if . . . ? I was thirteen years old, and yup, I can pinpoint the exact moment that my hillbilly entrepreneurship kicked in.

> I can pinpoint the exact moment that my hillbilly entrepreneurship kicked in.

I bought ten candy bars.

The next day, I took them to school in my lunch bag. When it came time for lunch, I got them out, and I offered them for sale to my friends at the table for 45 cents, profiting a dime from each candy bar and making myself $1 that day. I was off and running. It didn't hurt that the fifth graders were in the building, either, because those kids love sugar. When I was in eighth grade, my cousin was a fifth grader, and since we got on pretty well, I'm sure you can guess where this is going.

Now, the fifth graders didn't change classes like the sixth, seventh, and eighth graders, but it did so happen that my cousin and I had the same lunch period. Because of the way the campus was set up, gym classes were still held in the old high-school building. Yes, I know. Condemn the building but not the gym, and let kids still run loose in there? The '80s were truly a different time. The point is, you had to walk across the campus from the gym to the elementary building, and that's when I expanded my sugary empire, along with my fifth-grade cousin-slash-accomplice.

In an action to further protect the fragile health of us '80s kids, there was a Hi-C vending machine in the gym area. Not soda, because that would have been too unhealthy! Now, fifth graders didn't have open access to the Hi-C machine because they didn't move between classes and walked to the gym under teacher supervision. But not me, no. As an eighth grader, I was responsible for getting myself to PE class. This meant that I had access to the coveted Hi-C, available for the low, low price of 40 cents a can.

That's when my cousin and I struck the big deal. He would take drink orders on the bus after school each day, gather 55 cents from his customers, and give me the money in the morning. I'd buy the cans of Hi-C, stash them in my locker, and distribute them at our shared lunch period. His cut was 5 cents a can, mine was 10. We were becoming eleven- and fourteen-year-old logistics masters! We were marketing, taking orders, collecting profits, and moving products like seasoned professionals. And then, jealousy struck and, ultimately, became our downfall.

One of my cousin's classmates was a little envious about what my cousin was doing, but what he couldn't figure out was HOW my cousin was getting the Hi-C. The classmate decided that my cousin was somehow leaving the schoolroom, running across campus to the vending machine, and then running back with the cans in time to pass them around in the cafeteria. It's a decent deduction for a fifth grader, sure, but when he went to test out his theory, disaster befell us all. He didn't make it back to the lunchroom in time and confessed to the principal what he'd been trying to do. As a result, fifth graders were no longer allowed to drink Hi-C. That was the beginning of the end for my first entrepreneurial operation.

Never Lost That Drive

While my junior-high empire may have crumbled, I never did shake my hillbilly business sense. The problem was, while I was busy being, and slowly coming to resent being, a criminal defense lawyer, that spirit was lying a little dormant. It took sitting in the swampy heat of a courthouse hallway on a

Friday afternoon to flip that switch back on—much like that first "aha" moment with the candy bars when I was thirteen.

That's why I'm here; that's why I've told you these stories; and that's why I've written this book. It's the 21st century, and while I'm now a little older, a little wiser, and a little more technology driven than I was in the '80s, I want to share my hillbilly entrepreneurial spirit with you. So come along with me, the high-tech hillbilly lawyer, and I'll show you how to lose the suit, grow your law firm, and never have to set foot in a courtroom again.

CHAPTER 2

BURN YOUR LAWYER SUIT AND FIND THE FREEDOM MINDSET

Strap in, friends, because I'm set to drop a lot of truth on you about what's wrong with the traditional law profession, how technology disrupts it, and how we can make these things right so you can enjoy a more satisfying career. It's going to be a long ride, but I want to be sure you have a solid grasp of the status of our profession, and where you can take your practice, so you can ensure a steady stream of income without the stress of wearing a suit and sweltering in a courthouse hallway.

The Rise of the Mega Law Firm

Entering law school with the expectation of a financially rewarding career has been a common motivation for many aspiring lawyers throughout history. Historically, the legal profession held the promise of a good income and stable job prospects. However, the landscape of the legal industry has evolved significantly over the past two decades, leading to challenges and changes in the financial prospects for lawyers. The rise of mega law firms (and the emergence of online legal service providers, which we'll talk about shortly) have reshaped the legal market, impacting the traditional notion of a prosperous legal career.

> Historically, the legal profession held the promise of a good income and stable job prospects.

Here's how the development of mega law firms has influenced the financial rewards of practicing law:

- Mega law firms, with their vast resources and extensive networks, have captured a significant share of high-value legal work.
- The exorbitant fees charged by mega law firms can make legal services inaccessible for many individuals and smaller businesses.
- Legal representation becomes a privilege reserved for those with substantial financial resources, leaving less-affluent clients with limited options or forced to settle for subpar legal assistance. This can perpetuate inequalities in accessing justice and legal representation.

While these concerns are significant enough on their own, they can snowball into even bigger issues, the gist of which is that these mega-firms can begin to focus on profit over justice. When financial gain becomes the primary motivation, some firms might be tempted to take on cases primarily for their profitability rather than their merit. This can compromise the principles of the legal profession and may lead to inadequate representation for certain clients. As lawyers, we need to be keenly aware of any negative impacts on the ethics of our chosen profession.

The influence of these mega-firms and their affluent and prominent clientele can also lead to undue influence on legal decision-making. The financial clout of these firms and their high-profile clients can potentially sway legal proceedings in favor of corporate interests, raising concerns about the fairness and impartiality of the legal system. Are you sensing a pattern here? Mega law firms are responsible for a cascading effect on the integrity of the law profession, and if you're a solo or small practitioner, you're standing at the bottom of the waterfall getting dumped on.

> If you're a solo or small practitioner, you're standing at the bottom of the waterfall getting dumped on.

The dominance of mega law firms in the legal market can overshadow smaller firms and solo practitioners. Smaller legal practices may struggle to compete with the vast resources and prestige of mega-firms, leading to a concentration of legal services within a select group of firms. This can limit the diversity of legal representation available to clients and reduce opportunities for small firms to thrive. There are some unhealthy potential reactions to losing your client base to the mega-firms.

One of those scenarios is the potential for overbilling and fee padding. With the emphasis on generating high revenue in an environment that prioritizes financial rewards, there might be a temptation to maximize billable hours and charge excessive fees. This behavior undermines the trust between lawyers and clients, and damages the reputation of the legal profession. The other harmful scenario is that small-practice attorneys may succumb to the pressure to handle complex and high-value cases, leading to an unsustainable workload. The pursuit of financial success may come at the cost of lawyers' well-being, leading to burnout, stress, and compromised work-life balance. This can have adverse effects on the quality of legal services provided and the overall satisfaction of legal professionals in their careers.

While mega law firms charging premium fees for specialized services may benefit a select group of lawyers financially, there are significant negative implications associated with this model. The inaccessibility of legal services for many clients, the potential compromises in the pursuit of justice, and the impact on smaller firms and solo practitioners are all concerning aspects of this trend. The legal profession must find a balance between financial success and its commitment to providing fair and equitable legal representation for all individuals and businesses. Emphasizing ethical practice, affordability, and equal access to justice should be at the forefront of efforts to address the challenges posed by the dominance of mega law firms in the legal industry.

The Advent of Online Legal Service Providers

The advent of online legal service providers has transformed the delivery of certain legal services, commoditizing some routine legal work. This expands on the existing problem of online platforms offering standardized legal documents and basic legal services at lower costs. As you'll see, it's not necessarily the cost that's the issue but the standardization. Legal matters should never be one-size-fits-all.

This leads to some worry about the quality and expertise offered by online providers:

- Online legal platforms may lack the specialized expertise and personalized advice that traditional legal practitioners can offer.
- While these platforms provide generic legal documents, they may not address the unique needs and circumstances of individual clients.
- As a result, clients using these services might not receive comprehensive or accurate legal guidance, potentially leading to legal complications and disputes down the line.

This can lead to an increase in legal errors because self-serve legal documents and limited guidance can cause clients to make mistakes. These documents can be complex and legally binding, so making any errors or omissions is potentially costly and time-consuming to rectify. Without the oversight of a skilled attorney, clients may face legal challenges that could have been prevented with proper legal advice.

The platforms are also plagued by a limited scope of services. Online platforms typically offer standardized templates for basic legal needs, excluding more intricate or nuanced legal matters. While these platforms might be suitable for simple legal tasks, they cannot address complex situations that require customized solutions. As a result, clients may believe their legal needs are met when, in reality, they may require more comprehensive and tailored assistance. Online platforms cannot provide legal representation in court or handle adversarial proceedings, and clients need experienced attorneys who can advocate on their behalf.

Online platforms lack the capability to offer such representation, limiting their scope to transactional or non-litigious matters.

There is also a lack of personalized support with online platforms. Traditional legal practitioners offer a deeper level of engagement with clients, taking the time to understand their specific concerns and providing tailored advice. Online platforms lack this personalized approach, potentially leaving clients feeling unsupported in critical legal matters. Alongside the impact on clients, the proliferation of online legal services has intensified competition and price pressure for traditional legal practitioners. As clients turn to online platforms for cost-effective solutions, traditional lawyers may face challenges in attracting and retaining clients. This, in turn, can reduce their income potential, especially in areas where online services have gained popularity.

> The proliferation of online legal services has intensified competition and price pressure for traditional legal practitioners.

While online legal platforms appear to offer cost-effective solutions for basic legal needs, they come with substantial drawbacks and limitations. Clients using these services must be cautious about the quality and accuracy of the legal documents they receive. For more complex legal matters or situations requiring personalized advice, traditional legal practitioners remain essential. To address the income reduction faced by traditional lawyers due to online competition, legal professionals may need to focus on providing value-added services, emphasizing their expertise, personalized support, and ability to handle complex legal matters.

Additionally, collaboration between traditional lawyers and online platforms could offer a balanced approach, providing clients with a range of options and ensuring that their legal needs are met effectively and professionally. Ultimately, the legal profession must adapt to the changing landscape and find innovative ways to provide accessible, reliable, and high-quality legal services to clients in an increasingly digital era. Until then, as legal services become more commoditized, more clients are becoming increasingly price-conscious, seeking cost-effective alternatives for their legal needs. This shift in client behavior can significantly impact the financial viability of smaller practices.

Understanding the Challenges Faced by Small Practitioners

Let's take a look at the many pressures faced by solo practitioners and smaller firms due to the rise of mega-firms and online legal providers. Larger firms can spread their fixed costs over a larger client base, enabling them to offer competitive pricing while still maintaining profitability. On the other hand, smaller practices may struggle to match these lower prices due to their higher overhead expenses relative to the number of clients they serve. Beyond these economic factors, there are several other challenges that small practices can face.

The first of these are marketing and branding challenges. Establishing a strong brand presence and marketing a smaller legal practice can present a significant obstacle. Mega law firms

> Mega law firms and online providers have the advantage of widespread brand recognition and extensive marketing budgets.

and online providers have the advantage of widespread brand recognition and extensive marketing budgets. This visibility attracts a steady stream of clients, making it difficult for smaller firms to compete for a share of the market.

Technology and automation may also prove to be a challenge for small firms. Online legal platforms use these innovations to streamline their processes and reduce costs. Automation allows online providers to offer standardized services efficiently, cutting down on manual labor and administrative overhead. Smaller firms may find it challenging to adopt similar technologies due to the associated implementation costs.

The increasing presence of mega-firms and online platforms can warp clients' perception of the value of your services. As legal services become more commoditized, clients may perceive that all legal providers offer similar services, regardless of their size or specialization. This perception of homogeneity can lead clients to prioritize cost over other factors when selecting a legal provider. Smaller firms that offer specialized expertise and personalized attention may struggle to convey the unique value they bring to their clients.

Overcoming These Challenges

While it can feel at times that mega-firms and online legal platforms are taking over, please know that there are things you can do to combat the negative impacts on your business. First, you can adapt service offerings to meet the changing demands of clients in the digital age. Clients increasingly seek convenience, accessibility, and efficiency in their legal services. Smaller firms must find ways to offer innovative and tech-savvy solutions without compromising on the quality and personal touch that sets them apart.

You can also consider collaboration and niche specialization; this can provide you with a competitive edge. By forming alliances or networks, smaller firms can pool resources and expertise, offering clients a wider range of services. Niche specialization allows them to become experts in specific areas of law, attracting clients seeking specialized assistance.

Smaller law firms and solo practitioners face significant financial challenges in a legal landscape where pricing pressures are increasing, and online legal services are gaining popularity. To thrive in this environment, these practices must focus on their unique strengths, such as personalized attention, specialized expertise, and niche specializations. Embracing technology and finding creative ways to adapt to changing client demands will be essential.

Additionally, fostering collaborative relationships with other practitioners and leveraging their combined resources can help level the playing field. The legal profession must recognize the diverse needs of clients and continue to evolve to provide accessible, efficient, and high-quality legal services, ensuring the financial viability of smaller practices in an increasingly competitive market.

OTHER CONCERNS WITH THE LEGAL PROFESSION TODAY

The rise of mega-firms and online platforms isn't the only concern for lawyers these days. The growth of law-school enrollments and the number of law graduates has led to increased competition for legal positions. The saturation of the legal job market isn't only a challenge for newly graduated lawyers; it also affects existing and older practitioners. As the legal industry evolves and faces various economic and technological shifts, seasoned lawyers may encounter unique challenges that impact their financial stability and career progression.

Job-market saturation also increases the competition for clients, impacting the ability of existing practitioners to attract and retain a steady clientele. Seasoned lawyers who have relied on established client bases may find it challenging to compete with younger, tech-savvy attorneys who leverage online marketing and social media to reach new clients. Maintaining a consistent flow of clients becomes crucial for sustaining financial stability.

The pressure to maintain a consistent client base is accompanied by the pressure to stay relevant. With technological advancements and changing client expectations, experienced lawyers may feel pressure to update their skills and knowledge continuously. Staying relevant in the legal industry requires continuous learning and adaptation to new legal technologies and trends. Lawyers who fail to keep up may find it difficult to compete and retain clients, potentially leading to reduced income and financial strain. That can lead to yet another concern, which is the ability to retire. As the legal job market becomes more competitive, older practitioners may postpone retirement due to financial uncertainties.

Some experienced lawyers may wish to retire or scale back their practices, but concerns about financial stability and retirement savings may deter them from doing so. This can lead to burnout and impact overall job satisfaction. As the legal market

> This can lead to burnout and impact overall job satisfaction.

becomes more competitive, older lawyers may feel compelled to work longer hours to maintain their position in the industry. The pressure to compete and secure clients can lead to an imbalance between work and personal life, impacting overall well-being and job satisfaction.

A shift in client preferences and market demands, which is still yet *another* concern, may alter the focus of legal services sought by clients. Established lawyers with expertise in areas that experience reduced demand may need to diversify their practice or transition to other legal specializations. This transition can be financially challenging, especially if it requires additional training or certifications. Meanwhile, alternative billing methods and online legal services can cause clients to exert pressure on experienced lawyers to lower their fees. Clients seeking more cost-effective options may negotiate lower fees or seek services from online providers, potentially reducing the income potential of established practitioners.

To summarize this laundry list... why the heck would you want to be a lawyer these days?

What Should Lawyers Be Doing?

The saturation of the legal job market presents challenges not only for newly graduated lawyers but also for experienced practitioners. To navigate these challenges, existing lawyers must stay adaptable, continuously improve their skills, and remain responsive to changing client demands and market trends. Embracing technology and innovative legal solutions can help seasoned lawyers maintain their competitiveness and financial stability in an increasingly dynamic legal landscape. Additionally, fostering a strong professional network and seeking mentorship opportunities can provide valuable support and guidance throughout their legal careers. By proactively addressing the issues associated with a saturated job market, experienced lawyers can position themselves for continued success and financial security. There are also some other considerations for lawyers of all ages to improve their practices and profits.

Consider your practice's technology. Advancements have automated certain legal tasks and reduced the demand for traditional legal services. This rapid advancement is revolutionizing the legal industry, creating both challenges and opportunities for lawyers of all experience levels. To thrive in this dynamic landscape, legal practitioners must embrace legal tech and adapt their skills to meet the evolving needs of clients. Here's how embracing technology and focusing on specialized areas of practice can enhance the earning potential of lawyers.

Legal tech tools, such as case management software, document automation, and artificial intelligence, streamline legal processes and enhance productivity. By incorporating these tools into their practices, lawyers can handle cases more efficiently, allowing them to take on a higher caseload and increase their earning potential without sacrificing quality. Embracing legal tech can enhance lawyers' ability to engage in targeted marketing and business-development efforts.

> Satisfied clients are more likely to refer others to a lawyer.

Using technology to improve client communication and collaboration can also lead to higher client satisfaction. Satisfied clients are more likely to refer others to a lawyer, resulting in a steady stream of referrals and continued business growth.

Technology has also expanded the reach of legal services, allowing lawyers to access clients beyond their immediate geographic location. Lawyers can tap into specialized niches or cater to niche markets that may not have been accessible before. This expansion increases the pool of potential clients and revenue streams. Technology also allows lawyers to offer new and innovative service-delivery models, such as virtual consultations or online legal platforms. By offering flexible and convenient services, lawyers can attract a broader client base and potentially charge premium fees for added convenience. By leveraging digital marketing strategies and data analytics, lawyers can also identify and connect with potential clients more effectively, leading to increased opportunities for new business.

Focusing on specialized areas of practice allows lawyers to become experts in their field, setting them apart from general practitioners. We're going to spend a ton of time focusing on specialization in the rest of this book. I don't want you to fear specialization though. While some might tell you that it's a great way to pigeonhole yourself, I'm here to tell you that it can set you free. Clients often seek specialized expertise for complex legal matters, and lawyers with a proven track record in specific areas can command higher fees and attract more high-value cases.

The Bottom Line Before We Move On

In a technology-driven legal landscape, embracing legal tech and focusing on specialized areas of practice are essential steps for lawyers looking to enhance their earning potential. By leveraging technology to improve efficiency, expand their reach, and offer innovative services, lawyers can attract a broader client base and command higher fees. Specialization allows lawyers to become experts in their field, setting them apart from the competition and attracting high-value cases.

As the legal industry continues to evolve, adapting to new technologies and embracing innovation will be key to thriving as a lawyer in this dynamic and competitive environment.

The financial prospects of practicing law have undergone significant shifts over the past twenty years. While some lawyers continue to thrive in mega-firms and specialized practices, others face challenges due to increased competition, online legal service providers, and evolving client expectations. The legal profession's financial rewards are no longer a guarantee, and aspiring lawyers must be prepared to navigate a dynamic and competitive landscape. Adapting to changing market conditions, embracing technology, and focusing on areas of expertise can help lawyers find success and financial fulfillment in a profession that remains valuable but demands flexibility and innovation. Ultimately, a career in law can still be financially rewarding for those who approach it with a strategic mindset and a willingness to evolve with the times.

In many ways, it's a self-inflicted wound. The legal industry is usually the very last to adopt or implement any type of innovation or technology, the last to evolve with the times, and is highly resistant to change. Because of this, many lawyers are trapped in old ways of thinking about our profession and the way things should be done. One of the best things you can do for your practice and yourself is something we haven't even touched upon yet, and that's alternative billing models. Technology facilitates the implementation of alternative billing models, such as flat fees or subscription-based services. These billing models offer transparency and predictability to clients while allowing lawyers to set competitive rates based on the value of their services.

In the next chapter, we'll explore alternative billing methods in depth, and I'll share with you my first attempt at revolutionizing my own practice, long before I hit my limit sitting in a muggy courthouse hallway. Stick with me, friends, and discover how to lose the suit, once and for all.

CHAPTER 3

CHANGE YOUR BILLING AND CHANGE YOUR LIFE

One of the sacred cows that needs to be sacrificed for the good of the profession is hourly billing. But when I talk to lawyers about moving away from this model, I rarely find any willingness to even discuss it, let alone to implement a change. Here's a secret: I don't charge by the hour—never have.

Think about it. How is hourly billing good for anyone? It immediately creates a divided interest between the lawyer and the client. For the client, it presents a daunting problem of a potentially unknown and unbearable legal bill. The client wants the best representation, for the lowest price. Should their lawyer work on their case (and bill them) for many hours? Does that mean the representation is good? What should the lawyer do? Work (and bill) for as few hours as possible, just enough to do the bare minimum so the client won't argue about the bill? It's an untenable situation, and the legal industry has just ignored it.

Hourly billing immediately pits the lawyer AGAINST their own client, and that needs to end. The lawyer's financial gain is directly tied to the number of billable hours worked, which can lead to a potential conflict of interest. Clients may worry that their lawyer is incentivized to prolong legal matters to increase billable hours rather than resolving the case efficiently.

> Hourly billing immediately pits the lawyer AGAINST their own client, and that needs to end.

THIS IS A PROBLEM FOR EVERYONE

Hourly billing presents a tremendous problem for everyone involved, and let's break down why.

Uncertain and Unpredictable Costs: Hourly billing can create uncertainty for clients regarding the total cost of legal services. The unpredictability of accumulating legal fees can be overwhelming and may lead clients to avoid seeking legal assistance altogether, even when they genuinely need it.

Pressure to Minimize Hours: Clients may fear that their lawyer will work on their case for as few hours as possible to keep costs down, potentially compromising the quality of representation. This pressure to minimize billable hours can lead to rushed work and less attention to detail, ultimately impacting the client's case.

Billing Disputes: Hourly billing can lead to billing disputes and strained lawyer-client relationships. Clients may question the reasonableness of billed hours or feel uncomfortable raising concerns about the bill, fearing it could negatively impact the quality of representation.

Inefficiency and Time-Tracking Concerns: For lawyers, hourly billing can be time-consuming and may distract from the core legal work. Tracking every minute spent on a case can be cumbersome, and the focus on billable hours may overshadow the importance of providing value and achieving favorable outcomes for clients.

Limited Transparency: Hourly billing may lack transparency, making it challenging for clients to understand how their legal fees are calculated. Clients may be left wondering what specific tasks were performed and whether they were necessary for their case.

Incentive to Overwork: On the flip side, hourly billing can create an incentive for some lawyers to overwork to increase billable hours, potentially leading to burnout and diminished work-life balance.

Hourly billing has inherent drawbacks that can create a disconnect between lawyers and clients, leading to concerns about cost, transparency, and the quality of representation. As a result, many legal professionals and clients have recognized the need for alternative billing models, such as flat-fee value billing or other innovative fee structures. These approaches focus on providing clients with clear, predictable costs while encouraging lawyers to prioritize value-driven outcomes rather than the number of hours worked. By moving away from hourly billing, the legal industry can address these concerns and foster a more collaborative and transparent relationship between lawyers and clients.

For the lawyer, hourly billing is a bad deal. The national average was $269/hour in 2022. If a lawyer could bill forty hours a week for fifty-two weeks a year, their maximum gross is only $559,520. Take out one-third for overhead, and we're down to $373,013.33. Then pay taxes. Suddenly it doesn't look like that lucrative a career. And that's if you get your full billing. Part of a firm? They get their cut. It's just not as lucrative as most lawyers hoped—until they can crawl to the top of the heap and start taking a share of what some junior lawyers in their firm are earning.

Perception vs. Reality

Despite the perception that practicing law can be financially rewarding, hourly billing can make it difficult for lawyers to achieve the level of income they might have anticipated. It creates an income ceiling that isn't easy to see until you hit it. The reality is that hourly billing places a cap on a lawyer's earning potential, as their income is directly tied to the number of billable hours they can work in a given week or year. This can limit their ability to increase their earnings significantly unless they consistently work long hours, leading to potential burnout.

Hourly billing also comes with time-consuming administrative tasks that require lawyers to meticulously track their time and prepare detailed invoices, which can take away from billable work. The administrative burden can also detract from focusing on clients and delivering high-quality legal services. Plus, the pressure to bill more hours can lead to a focus on quantity over quality, with lawyers potentially sacrificing the time needed to thoroughly address a client's legal needs to meet billing targets.

Junior lawyers may face difficulties in accumulating billable hours, making it challenging for them to generate sufficient income to cover their expenses and loans from law school. In larger firms, this problem becomes magnified. Large law firms or partners often have a higher hourly rate, leading to significant disparities in earning potential between junior and senior lawyers. This can create an inequitable internal compensation structure. Not to mention that certain tasks, such as research, preparation, and client communication, may not always be billable hours, leading to the potential for uncompensated work.

As a result of these issues, many lawyers are seeking alternative billing models, such as flat-fee value billing or subscription-based services, to provide clients with greater transparency and to prioritize value-driven outcomes. By moving away from hourly billing and embracing more client-centric fee structures, lawyers can improve their financial prospects, focus on delivering high-quality legal services, and create a more sustainable and fulfilling legal career.

Focus on Efficiency and Alternative Billing Models

Clients' demands for efficiency and transparency have prompted lawyers to explore alternative billing models, such as flat fees and value-based billing. Adopting alternative billing methods in the legal industry has the potential to bring numerous advantages to both clients and lawyers. However, implementing these new approaches may necessitate firms reevaluating their financial structures and adapting to evolving client expectations.

Alternative billing methods, such as flat fees or subscription-based models, offer clients greater transparency and predictability

> Clients appreciate the certainty of knowing the exact cost of legal services upfront.

in legal costs. Clients appreciate the certainty of knowing the exact cost of legal services upfront, allowing them to budget more effectively. For law firms, this requires careful estimation and assessment of the work involved in each case to establish fair and competitive pricing.

Alternative billing methods can align the interests of clients and lawyers, fostering a collaborative and mutually beneficial relationship. Unlike traditional hourly billing, which may incentivize lawyers to prolong legal processes to increase billable hours, alternative methods prioritize efficiency and prompt resolution. This encourages lawyers to deliver quality results in a timely manner, reinforcing client satisfaction.

Law firms need to adapt their financial models to accommodate alternative billing methods. However, shifting away from a traditional hourly billing structure may require firms to modify their accounting practices and create new billing systems. This change necessitates careful planning and communication with both clients and internal teams. To effectively do this, firms also need to carefully consider risk management. Alternative billing methods may introduce new risk considerations for both clients and lawyers. Flat fees or performance-based billing can carry the risk of underestimating the work required for a particular case, potentially leading to financial losses. For clients, performance-based billing may create concerns about the quality of service or potential conflicts of interest.

As alternative billing methods become more prevalent, clients may come to expect greater pricing flexibility from legal service providers. Law firms may encounter client demands for alternative billing options, requiring them to assess their capacity to offer these arrangements. Striking a balance between accommodating client preferences and maintaining financial sustainability will be crucial. Communication also plays a crucial role in the transition away from hourly billing. Clients may be more likely to question the value they receive for their investment in legal services under alternative billing arrangements. Law firms must proactively communicate the benefits and outcomes of their services to reinforce the perceived value.

By proactively addressing the challenges and opportunities associated with alternative billing, law firms can position themselves to thrive in an evolving legal landscape, where client expectations continue to shift toward greater transparency and value-driven services.

The Flat-Fee Value Billing Model

A flat-fee value billing model solves all these problems. When the lawyer and client agree on the cost in advance, there's no anxiety for the client about the bill. The lawyer doesn't have to worry about spending too much or too little time on the case. And by billing for value, the lawyer can use technology and staff to create an unlimited income instead of being capped by how many billable hours they can squeeze out.

Flat-fee value billing provides not only financial freedom but also schedule freedom. Not being tied to billing hours allows the lawyer to focus on results rather than time billed. It no longer matters if the lawyer or the lower-billing-rate paralegal or legal secretary provides the service; the bill is the same. The lawyer leverages staff and technology to free up flexibility in their schedule and make

> Flat-fee value billing provides not only financial freedom but also schedule freedom.

time for family, hobbies, and an all-around better work-life balance.

A flat-fee value billing model can be a game changer for both lawyers and clients. This innovative approach addresses many of the challenges associated with hourly billing and offers numerous benefits for all parties involved. Let's take a dive into how a flat-fee value billing model can transform the legal industry.

Predictable Costs: With flat-fee value billing, the lawyer and client agree on the cost of legal services upfront. This transparency eliminates the anxiety and uncertainty associated with hourly billing, as clients know the total cost from the outset. Clients can confidently seek legal assistance without the fear of unexpected and escalating bills.

Focus on Value-Driven Outcomes: Billing for value allows lawyers to concentrate on delivering high-quality outcomes for their clients rather than on billable hours. Lawyers can invest the necessary time and effort to provide comprehensive and effective legal solutions without feeling constrained by time tracking.

Financial Freedom: By adopting a flat-fee value billing model, lawyers can break free from the income ceiling imposed by hourly billing. With no limitations from billable hours, lawyers can leverage their expertise, technology, and staff to handle multiple cases efficiently and increase their earning potential.

Flexibility and Work-Life Balance: Without the pressure of billing hours, lawyers can enjoy greater schedule freedom. They can allocate their time more effectively, delegate tasks to paralegals or legal secretaries without compromising income, and create a healthier work-life balance. This newfound flexibility allows lawyers to make time for personal pursuits, family, hobbies, and other interests.

Enhanced Client Relations: Flat-fee value billing fosters a stronger lawyer-client relationship built on trust and transparency. Clients appreciate knowing the exact cost of legal services in advance and feel more confident in their lawyer's dedication to achieving favorable results.

Leveraging Technology and Staff: By adopting a flat-fee value billing model, lawyers are encouraged to leverage technology and staff to improve efficiency and productivity. Automated processes, specialized software, and delegated tasks allow lawyers to handle more cases effectively.

Efficient Resource Allocation: With a clear understanding of the resources required for each case, lawyers can allocate their time, staff, and technology appropriately. This leads to optimal resource management, reducing overhead costs and increasing overall profitability.

A flat-fee value billing model offers a transformative approach to legal services that addresses the shortcomings of hourly billing. By providing predictable costs, focusing on value-driven outcomes, and fostering financial and schedule freedom, lawyers can create a more rewarding and fulfilling legal career. Additionally, clients benefit from transparency, enhanced lawyer-client relationships, and the confidence of knowing they are receiving high-quality legal representation without the fear of unexpected costs. Embracing this innovative billing model empowers lawyers to thrive in a dynamic legal landscape while prioritizing client needs and delivering outstanding legal services.

LOSE THE SUIT AND AVOID THE COURTHOUSE

While flat-fee value billing can be applied with certain tweaks and variations across all types of legal practice, for true freedom the lawyer also needs to be free from the court.

Spending time in court is almost always a value-negative prospect. For hourly billers, the client pays (sometimes at a premium rate) for their lawyer to sit—sometimes for hours—waiting for their case to be called, with the lawyer spending maybe a total of five to fifteen minutes actually presenting an argument to the court. Drive time is also normally billed to the client.

> For true freedom, the lawyer also needs to be free from the court.

When the court is involved, it's also an adversarial process. The lawyer is at the mercy of the judge on when to appear and at the mercy of opposing counsel, who can file and notice up motions, requiring a response and maybe an appearance, all to be billed to the client and taking away the lawyer's freedom from the calendar. Court appearances can be a significant drain on both the lawyer's and the client's resources, and they may not always align with the value-driven approach of flat-fee value billing.

For lawyers using flat-fee value billing, minimizing court time is a strategic move to maximize efficiency, enhance client relations, and provide cost-effective legal services. By embracing technological solutions and alternative dispute-resolution methods, lawyers can reduce the time spent in court while maintaining a focus on delivering value-driven outcomes for their clients. This approach not only benefits lawyers by allowing them more freedom from the calendar but also strengthens the lawyer-client relationship and promotes a more sustainable and successful legal practice.

Personal Experience with Value Billing

One of my first attempts at value billing was founding MissouriTrafficTickets.com, which was also one of my first attempts at using technology to have a more efficient practice and bring in a larger client base. When I launched the website in 2002, it was the first fully online legal platform in the world and was based on a model of helping people fight their traffic tickets without the hassle of hourly billing, going to court, or facing losing down points on their licenses, or worse. It was and remains a fairly simple process: tell us about your ticket; we tell you what can be done about it; and then we do it! If I could go to court for only a couple of hours a day, resolve a couple of dozen traffic tickets, get paid $75 a ticket, AND have happy clients, then there was no downside.

> One of my first attempts at value billing was founding MissouriTrafficTickets.com.

I sold my traffic tickets platform in 2020 to focus on other things, but I'm still so proud of that business. It was a groundbreaking concept, and I'll always be glad for the experience and the glimpse of freedom from suits and the courthouse that it gave me, even if that glimpse didn't grow to an even more exciting view until 2015. What happened after I saw things from a new vantage point is what we'll talk about in the next chapter, where I'll show you how changing your practice specialty can change your life. And trust me, you'll love the part where you never have to wear a suit again.

CHAPTER 4

THE ESTATE PLANNING SECRET

When I first got into the legal game, picking the right niche was crucial. I figured that I needed to find a pond that had a lot of fish in it. As a criminal defense attorney, I noticed that I was serving only a small fraction of the population. Because of that, I faced the challenge of having a regular flow of clients and income.

I also handled traffic tickets, but I faced the same problem. Most people only get one or two in a lifetime. That would never allow me to have a thriving practice. I peeked into the divorce arena, but I wasn't up for the stress or emotion—I mean that of both the clients and myself. It all just seemed too draining.

What about business law? Yes, it offered a bigger swath of daily clients, but again, there just weren't enough businesses that faced complex legal issues for me to grow my practice steadily. I kept looking. I wanted to find an area of law where there was a steady demand—one that would give me a chance to positively impact these clients' lives.

Finding My Niche

While I was hunting for my new specialty, I felt drawn again and again to estate planning. We've all known someone who passed away without their affairs in order, and we've seen the mess it can leave behind for their loved ones. The more I thought about it, the more I realized estate planning fit all my aspirations. Everyone, regardless of age, background, or financial status, can benefit from creating an estate plan to protect their assets and loved ones. And unlike criminal defense, divorce, or even business law, estate planning presented a near-unlimited pool of potential clientele.

> I felt drawn again and again to estate planning.

Aside from actually being able to find clients, I realized that once I had them, I could retain them! Estate planning is not a one-time engagement but an ongoing process requiring periodic reviews and updates. This aspect really appealed to me because it meant I could establish long-term relationships with my clients and become their trusted adviser throughout various stages of their lives.

I also loved that estate planning allowed me the chance to make a meaningful difference. It wasn't just a matter of assisting folks with paperwork and guiding their financial future. It was a reward in and of itself to see the peace of mind on people's faces once they knew that their estate plans were well structured and put in place. This shift from criminal defense gave me peace of mind too. I could now build long-term, trusted relationships with my clients instead of dealing with adversarial situations. Focusing on tailored solutions, trust, and collaboration significantly boosted my lawyer-client relationships. Adopting my new specialty was a win all around.

Modernizing the Process

As I was hunting my niche, I realized that I wasn't just looking for something to stabilize and sustain my career or better the lives of my clients. Those things were both true, sure, but I felt the unmistakable pull of looking for a project. You know that feeling, right? When you see something that's broken or at least not in its best condition, you want to find a way to improve it, fix it, make it stronger, and make it your own. Estate planning was that for me.

I recognized that, in and around my home area, estate planning was a bit of a fixer-upper. It was there, and it was adequate, but it wasn't being delivered with much excellence, efficiency, or value for the client. But I could see the potential—I saw the glimmer, and I saw something I could make my own that would set me apart.

> Estate planning was a bit of a fixer-upper.

If you want to be the best at something, you must have the right combination of tools and know-how. It's about having the skills and the equipment you need to get the job done, done well, and done well the first time. Early on in my estate planning journey, I realized the process was a bit broken down and outdated. I saw that I needed to leverage technology and adopt new approaches in order to fix the problems of inefficient and incomplete estate planning. I knew that if I embraced modern tools and strategies, I could *revolutionize* estate planning services.

One of the challenges that stood out to me in traditional estate planning practices was the reliance on manual paperwork and time-consuming processes. To combat that, I needed to integrate cutting-edge software and digital platforms. Using state-of-the-art estate planning software, I streamlined the creation and management of legal documents, making the process more efficient and reducing the chances of errors and omissions.

Those upgrades meant that I could offer my clients a secure and user-friendly portal where they could access their estate planning documents, review updates, and make changes whenever necessary. In turn, that gave them more control over their plans and allowed them to stay informed about any modifications to their estate planning as their circumstances evolved.

The companion to changing technology was changing my approach. No longer would one-size-fits-all estate planning be the default. In fact, I eliminated it completely with a personalized approach to every client's estate plan. I conducted in-depth consultations to understand their unique goals, family dynamics, and financial situation, allowing me to craft customized strategies tailored to their specific needs. I then kicked everything up another notch by emphasizing the importance of ongoing reviews and updates to estate plans. Life is ever-changing, and what may have been an ideal estate plan at one point may become outdated as circumstances shift. By encouraging regular check-ins with my clients, I ensured that their estate plans remained up-to-date and aligned with their current wishes and objectives.

There was one more piece of the puzzle for me when it came to modernizing the estate planning process, and that was education. I wanted to make it easy for my clients to learn and find additional resources, so I added workshops, webinars, and user-friendly educational materials. These resources opened up a whole new world of possibilities for my clients and potential clients, who are now excited to sit down and plan their futures, and make arrangements for their families' future generations.

By embracing technology and adopting innovative approaches, I was able to fix many, if not all, of the problems of inefficient and incomplete estate planning that had plagued the industry for years. My practice became known for its client-focused experience and for delivering exceptional value and results. We were even able to bring the initial turnaround time for estate planning down from four to six months to four to six weeks. Clients appreciated the convenience, transparency, and forward-thinking strategies that set my estate planning services apart from traditional practices, and I appreciated the privilege of being there for them on this journey.

> Clients appreciated the convenience, transparency, and forward-thinking strategies.

There's Value for Everyone in Estate Planning

Another compelling factor that drew me toward estate planning was the recognition that it is an area of high value, but it had fallen prey to commoditized legal products from online platforms like LegalZoom and others. While these platforms claim to get the job done, you do get what you pay for, and clients don't always get the results they want or expect. It's a hurdle that I was willing to jump to help estate planning retain its significance as a specialized and personalized service that requires the expertise of a knowledgeable professional.

You see, in many fields of law, estate planning among them, the rise of online legal service providers and mass-produced legal documents has led to a shift toward delivering services at the lowest possible cost, often compromising on the quality of the service provided. This commoditization of legal services can lead to a devaluation of the skills and expertise that legal professionals bring to the table.

Estate planning, however, remains an area where the unique circumstances and desires of each client demand a tailored and thoughtful approach. Each individual's or family's estate plan requires careful consideration of their financial assets, family dynamics, future aspirations, and long-term objectives. Cookie-cutter solutions simply do not suffice when it comes to securing one's financial future and protecting loved ones.

Choosing estate planning as my practice area allowed me to provide high-value services that go beyond the standard templates and form documents. By taking the time to truly understand my clients' needs and objectives, I could craft customized estate plans that addressed their specific concerns and offered the highest level of protection and peace of mind.

I also loved that estate planning inherently allowed me to be a continuous learner. As new tools and training arose, I got to move with the times and apply those skills to improve each client's experience. As an estate planning attorney, I was able to use my expertise to guide clients through intricate legal processes, offering comprehensive solutions that considered all aspects of their lives.

By focusing on estate planning, I avoided the trap of reducing my services to mere commodities. Instead, I emphasized the value of personalized attention, meticulous planning, and dedicated client care. This commitment to delivering high-value services distinguished my practice from those who opted for generic, one-size-fits-all approaches.

That Hourly Billing Thing Again

Avoiding hourly billing was a crucial consideration in my decision to focus on estate planning and steer clear of adversarial legal realms. As discussed in Chapter 2, hourly billing can create a host of challenges for both the lawyer and the client, leading to divided interests and potential disputes over billing. By moving away from hourly billing and adopting a flat-fee value billing model, I was able to provide a more transparent and predictable fee structure for my clients.

In adversarial areas of law, such as litigation or contentious legal matters, hourly billing can exacerbate the tension between the lawyer and the client. Clients may become anxious about the accumulating legal bills as the case progresses, and they may wonder if their lawyer is truly working in their best interest or simply trying to increase billable hours. Plus, opposing counsel may also engage in tactics that prolong the legal process, leading to a higher number of billable hours for both sides. As a result, the client may end up paying substantial fees without a clear resolution in sight. This adversarial approach can strain the client-lawyer relationship and create unnecessary conflicts.

By focusing on estate planning, which is a consultative and non-adversarial area of law, I could avoid these issues associated with hourly billing. Estate planning involves collaboration between the lawyer and the client to create comprehensive strategies that align with the client's wishes and objectives. Instead of battling against opposing counsel, the focus is on providing thoughtful and personalized guidance. In an estate planning practice, the flat-fee value billing model aligns perfectly with the non-adversarial nature of the work. Clients know the cost in advance, eliminating any surprises or anxiety over the final bill. This model allows me to concentrate on providing exceptional service and value to my clients, knowing that my compensation is based on delivering high-quality estate planning solutions.

Financial and Calendar Freedom

By focusing on estate planning and avoiding adversarial areas, I have the freedom to prioritize results and outcomes rather than billable hours. This approach allows me to allocate my time and resources efficiently, ensuring that my clients receive the best possible service without unnecessary delays or conflicts.

The potential for recurring income was another significant consideration in my decision to focus on estate planning. Unlike certain practice areas where legal services are often one-time transactions, or are reliant on sporadic cases, estate planning allows for the establishment of ongoing relationships with clients. Estate planning is a continuous process, and clients often require periodic reviews and updates to their estate plans as their circumstances change. This creates opportunities for a lawyer to offer retainer-based services, providing clients with the assurance that their estate plans remain up-to-date and relevant.

To keep the cycle going by offering ongoing retainer services, I could maintain a steady stream of income without needing to constantly seek new clients or engage in time-consuming and unpredictable case-based work. These retainer arrangements may cover services such as regular estate plan reviews, updating legal documents, providing legal advice on financial matters, or offering guidance on charitable-giving strategies.

I also take full advantage of advancements in legal technology and automation, meaning certain aspects of estate planning can be streamlined. This allows me to provide efficient and cost-effective services to my clients. Routine administrative tasks, document preparation, and client communication can be handled by dedicated legal assistants or through automated systems, reducing the impact on my time while maintaining a high level of service.

By leveraging technology and delegating certain tasks, I could free up more time to focus on strategic planning and strengthening client relationships. I love that this methodology enhances my ability to serve my existing clients effectively but also provides me with the flexibility to explore additional opportunities for growth and expansion within the estate planning realm.

And for me, the final factor was no suits, and that meant no courtrooms. Estate planning offered me a way to have a legal career without the need to dress up in suits every day or spend hours in courtrooms dealing with contentious stuff. Instead, it's all about sitting down with clients, having open conversations, and finding personalized solutions to protect their assets and loved ones.

By going this route, I can be more casual in how I dress, and it's way less stressful than dealing with courtroom drama. I get to focus on building strong relationships with clients, understanding their needs, and providing them with the best estate planning services possible. In the end, estate planning gives me the freedom to be myself, ditch the suits, and enjoy a more laid-back and client-focused legal career. It's all about making a positive impact on people's lives without the formalities and hassles of courtrooms.

Estate planning, for me, was a clear winner when it came to choosing a new specialty. No hourly billing, more financial freedom, a terrific value proposition for a wide client base, better automation, stronger client relationships, and NO SUITS. It makes me one happy lawyer, that's for sure. If a client ever asks about my attire (often jeans and a T-shirt), I always tell them, "I don't buy expensive suits, and I pass the savings on to you!"

Like all law specialties, there was and is room for improvement. Education is so important to me because so many people are stuck on the myths that estate planning is only for the ultra-wealthy (which the heck it is not!) and that it's a long, complicated web of processes that are too expensive and too out of reach to undertake. Most people fear estate planning because they don't understand estate planning. I aim to help change those misperceptions along the way and help create new opportunities for people to learn more, plan their estates, and have greater understanding and control of their families' futures. And I'm here to tell you that you and your practice can do the same.

> "I don't buy expensive suits, and I pass the savings on to you!"

CHAPTER 5

SYSTEMS AND SCALABILITY

As we talked about earlier, hourly billing is inherently income-limiting, but so is any billing model if it lacks the systems to maximize attorney and staff time. A good system has three main components: (1) it limits the amount of time attorneys spend per case, (2) it limits the amount of time staff spends on routine tasks, and (3) it provides an enhanced sense of client engagement. Why is this so critical? Systems and scalability are the key factors in freedom of schedule and unlimited earning potential. Let's discuss how a good billing system makes the most of your time and resources.

IT'S ALL ABOUT OPTIMIZATION

When it comes to your practice, what I'm focused on is showing you how to work

> How to work smarter, not harder.

smarter, not harder. I want you to find financial freedom, more time in your planner, and fewer suits in your closet. To do that, you need to optimize your resources and set boundaries to ensure that you can achieve and maintain your practice—and do it on your own terms. A chat about the three items I listed above is in order.

Firstly, limiting the amount of time attorneys spend on each case is crucial. By having clear processes and guidelines in place, attorneys can work more efficiently and avoid getting bogged down in unnecessary tasks. This means focusing on high-value activities and delegating routine or administrative work to capable staff members.

Secondly, optimizing staff time is equally important. Implementing streamlined workflows and using technology to automate routine tasks can save valuable hours for both attorneys and support staff. By reducing time spent on repetitive work, staff can concentrate on more personal and client-focused aspects of the practice, contributing to overall productivity.

Finally, client engagement is a critical component of any successful system. Building strong connections with clients fosters trust and loyalty, leading to long-term relationships and potential referrals. Through regular communication, personalized attention, and understanding of clients' unique needs, the practice can deliver exceptional service that sets it apart from competitors.

In essence, a well-designed system addresses the limitations of any billing model by optimizing time and resources across the board. By empowering attorneys and staff to work more efficiently, the practice can take on more cases without sacrificing quality. Additionally, the enhanced focus on client engagement not only benefits the clients but also contributes to a positive reputation for the practice, attracting more clients over time. So, it's not just about the billing model; it's about creating a comprehensive system that allows the practice to thrive, providing value to clients while maximizing income potential for the attorneys and staff.

THE RIGHT TOOLS FOR THE JOB

I'm always on the lookout for new and better tools to plug into my system. Fortunately, there are a lot of people out there making some great tools. On the flip side, there are, unfortunately, a lot of people out there making terrible tools or tools of limited use. Sometimes, a really great tool will come along and replace three or four tools I'm currently using, and that's terrific. But sometimes, tools with one great feature will be integrated with two or three other features that are subpar and locked together, making the great tool useless for a system. A good tool should seamlessly integrate into your existing system without requiring excessive customization, making the implementation process smooth and efficient.

Each lawyer has their unique preferences and comfort level with technology. Some may be tech savvy and enjoy customizing tools to suit their specific workflow, while others may prefer a ready-to-use solution that requires minimal setup. The key is to select tools that align with your needs and preferences, ensuring they enhance your productivity rather than become a burden. For those who are confident in their tech skills, customizability can be a significant advantage, allowing these tech-savvy lawyers to tailor the tools precisely to their requirements. On the other hand, those less familiar with

> Select tools that align with your needs and preferences.

technology can opt for user-friendly tools with intuitive interfaces that are easy to navigate and implement.

Hiring a professional to assist with tool selection and implementation is a smart move for lawyers who may not have the time or expertise to handle these tasks themselves. Technology consultants or legal tech experts can help identify the most suitable tools for your practice and ensure a seamless integration process. This way, you can harness the full potential of the tools without the stress of navigating the tech landscape alone.

Furthermore, ongoing support and training are crucial to ensure that both you and your team can use the tools effectively. Whether you choose to handle the implementation yourself or seek professional assistance, investing in training sessions can empower everyone in your practice to make the most of the tools and optimize your workflow.

In the end, whether you prefer to customize tools to fit your exact needs or seek out user-friendly, ready-to-use solutions, the goal is to select tools that improve efficiency, enhance client service, and contribute to the overall success of your practice. By striking the right balance and leveraging technology effectively, you can elevate your practice and stay ahead in the ever-evolving legal landscape.

As an aside, don't be a Luddite. Several times during my career, a colleague would ask me to go for lunch or coffee to pick my brain about how I could accomplish so much without seeming rushed. Sometimes I'd be able to share and help, but more often than not, as soon as I'd mention a computer, piece of software, or the internet—they'd shut down.

> Don't be a Luddite.

"I'm not a technology person," they'd say. Then I can't really help you, I'd think. You have to be willing to learn.

Technology in the legal profession has been here for over three decades now (despite how hard so many lawyers resisted it), and it can't be ignored if you really want to succeed. While some of the higher-level intricacies can be handed off to staff or a contracted professional, you'll have to bite the bullet and become at least passingly acquainted with the tools you'll need every day to achieve your productivity goals.

I am a tech person. I have that advantage. I took and passed six exams through self-study in the late '90s to earn a fairly coveted Microsoft Certified Systems Engineer (MCSE) designation. And then I took three more to earn the +I (+Internet; it was optional back then) for the even more elite MCSE+I certification—basically for fun. Because I'm a tech kind of guy, integrating all these "newfangled" tools into my practice came easily to me. I get that it's not that easy for everyone, but it is essential.

The Dreaded Phone Call

The number one productivity killer for lawyers is the phone. In hourly billing, sure, it's great—make a phone call and bill the time, but remember you only have so much time to bill. For a systems-based practice, phone calls are anathema. While they can be essential for communication

> The number one productivity killer for lawyers is the phone.

and client relations, they can also be a significant productivity killer if not managed effectively. Why are phone calls so terrible?

Uni-Tasking vs. Multitasking: Phone calls indeed demand someone's undivided attention, making it challenging to multitask effectively. For lawyers with multiple responsibilities and tasks to handle, being tied up on the phone can disrupt their workflow and lead to delays in other essential matters. The inability to multitask efficiently can hamper productivity and create a backlog of pending tasks.

Time-Wasting Nature: Phone calls can consume a significant amount of time, especially if clients engage in prolonged discussions that could be handled more efficiently through other means. Additionally, if the information exchanged during the call requires research or further investigation, it may lead to follow-up communications and additional time investment.

Communication Challenges: Spoken communication over the phone has inherent limitations, as there is no recorded transcript of the conversation. This can lead to misunderstandings, misinterpretations, or clients misremembering the information shared during the call. Such miscommunication can potentially create disputes or disagreements later on, complicating the attorney-client relationship.

Given these problems that phone calls create, lawyers in systems-based practices may prefer and should encourage alternative forms of communication and client engagement:

Secure Electronic Communication: Encouraging clients to communicate through secure electronic communication allows for written documentation of exchanges, ensuring clarity and providing a reference for future discussions. Secure electronic communication also allow lawyers to respond thoughtfully after reviewing the necessary information, enhancing the accuracy and completeness of their responses. Secure electronic communication also can't be overheard, eliminating any confidentiality concerns a client may have about verbal conversations.

Client Portals: Using secure client portals enables clients to access relevant documents and information, reducing the need for lengthy phone calls. Clients can upload required documents and receive case updates through the portal, streamlining the communication process.

Video Conferencing: For more in-depth discussions or consultations, video conferencing can be a valuable alternative to phone calls. Video calls enable face-to-face interactions, which can help build rapport and understanding between lawyers and clients.

FAQ Resources: Creating a comprehensive FAQ section on the firm's website can address common client queries and concerns, providing a resource for clients to find answers to routine questions without the need for direct phone contact.

Set Specific Call Hours: Designate specific times during the day when you will take and return phone calls. This allows you to structure your day more efficiently and dedicate uninterrupted time to other essential tasks.

Use Virtual Receptionists or Call Screening Services: Use virtual receptionists or call screening services to manage incoming calls. They can filter calls, prioritize urgent matters, and provide essential information to clients, reducing the need for direct phone contact.

Use Voicemail Strategically: Set up a professional voicemail message that informs callers about your availability and when they can expect a call back. This way, clients know your call hours and can leave messages without expecting an immediate response. I personally choose not to accept voicemails at all; my outgoing cell-phone message states this and encourages people to text me instead. If you have the luxury of doing the same, do it! It's a game changer.

Schedule Call-Back Times: Instead of returning calls as they come in, schedule specific call-back times during the day. This allows you to address multiple calls at once, minimizing interruptions to your workflow.

Delegate Nonessential Calls: If possible, delegate nonessential phone calls to support staff or virtual assistants. They can handle routine inquiries and administrative tasks, freeing up your time for more critical matters.

By implementing these strategies, lawyers can effectively manage phone calls and maintain a productive systems-based practice. While communication remains vital, finding a balance that minimizes interruptions and allows for focused, efficient work is key to optimizing productivity and delivering exceptional service to clients.

I 100 percent prefer electronic, written communication for all my client interactions. So much so that I've taken our office phone number off my business cards and my website. I don't want phone calls. You see, phone calls are *synchronous communication.* They occur in real time. You talk, then I talk; you talk, then I talk; you talk... My response is required immediately after you speak. I call this the dreaded game of Stump the Lawyer.

> I've taken our office phone number off my business cards and my website.

It's so much better to get the questions in writing and have some leisure to find the time to craft a thoughtful and complete written response that the client can refer to in the future. That way, they won't have to call and ask the same question again next week when they've forgotten what I've told them on the phone. Phone calls interrupt the workflow. I'm in the middle of a project and—BAM—phone call. I have to stop in the middle of what I'm doing, refocus, handle the issues on the phone—in real time—and then try to refocus and get back on task. It's usually fifteen minutes of lost productivity in addition to the time spent on the phone.

People often tell me, "But it's so much easier just to call you and tell you!" My response is "For you!" It's easier because they want to dump a lot of information on me, and the phone call is the easiest way for them to do it. They can just rattle it all off, and it's my responsibility to accurately remember and record all the information—rather than them taking the responsibility to accurately put it all down in an email and send it. An email is something we can BOTH refer to if there's a misunderstanding. When people insist on a phone call, it's always for their benefit, not mine, and it's usually a transfer of responsibility to the lawyer's detriment. And honestly, I don't have, nor do I want to have, the mental bandwidth for that. I have better uses for my time and brain cells. I want to do everything I can to succeed and help my clients succeed, and phone calls just aren't conducive to that.

COMMUNICATION IS CRITICAL

No matter how you choose to communicate with your clients, it's essential to have systems in place that help you actively engage and support their needs. No one wants to feel like they aren't being heard. That's what we'll get to in the next chapter, so when you're ready, you can head on over there. I want to talk to you about finding the best ways to achieve a genuinely client-focused approach that will build robust, lasting relationships.

CHAPTER 6

STAYING FOCUSED ON THE CLIENTS

We spent a lot of time in the last few chapters talking about systems. How you run your practice has a tremendous impact on your efficiency, productivity, and income. But while great systems serve you well as the lawyer, great systems must also serve your clients, either directly or indirectly. The problem is there is a temptation to become so focused on our systems and our products that we fail to take the time to consider, let alone focus on, our clients and their needs. In this chapter, we'll spend time looking at all the ways you can continue to serve your own needs while ensuring that your clients always feel seen and heard.

PRIORITIZING NEEDS FOR BETTER OUTCOMES

Understanding and prioritizing the needs of clients is at the core of building strong and lasting relationships. Here's how adopting a client-focused approach can benefit lawyers and enhance the overall client experience:

Listening to Clients: Active listening and empathetic communication are crucial when understanding a client's needs. Lawyers should take the time to listen carefully to their clients' concerns, goals, and expectations. By doing so, they can gain valuable insights into the specific legal challenges their clients are facing.

Tailoring Solutions: Every client is unique, and their legal issues may require personalized solutions. A client-focused approach involves tailoring legal strategies to match the individual needs of each client. By providing customized solutions, lawyers can better address their clients' specific circumstances and achieve desired outcomes.

Using Plain Language: Clients want clarity and transparency in their legal matters. Lawyers should avoid using complex legal jargon and instead communicate in a language that clients can easily understand. Clear communication ensures that clients are well informed about their case's progress, potential challenges, and possible outcomes.

Being Results-Oriented: Clients are ultimately seeking results and resolutions to their legal problems. A client-focused lawyer concentrates on achieving positive outcomes for their clients rather than merely billing hours. This approach builds trust and confidence, as clients feel that their lawyer genuinely cares about their best interests.

In the field of estate planning law, a client-focused approach is particularly vital. Estate planning often involves making difficult and personal decisions about the distribution of assets after death, the designation of guardians for minor children, and the

> A client-focused approach is particularly vital.

creation of powers of attorney for health care and finances. These decisions can have a profound impact on the client and their loved ones. It is essential, therefore, that lawyers adopt a client-focused approach to ensure that the client's interests and wishes are at the forefront.

Managing Expectations Is Critical

In estate planning, there are a lot of moving parts, and even at your most productive, many things don't just happen overnight. You have to focus on your client's needs while also managing their expectations for services and timelines. There are several ways in which we can do this:

Clearly Explaining Processes: Estate planning involves a series of steps that might seem complex and overwhelming to clients. It is the lawyer's responsibility to explain the process clearly and honestly, providing a realistic overview of what to expect. This includes discussing the necessary documentation, legal requirements, potential tax implications, and the estimated time it takes to create a comprehensive estate plan.

Navigating Family Dynamics: Estate planning can sometimes involve challenging family dynamics or complex financial situations that could complicate the process. A client-focused approach requires lawyers to discuss these potential difficulties openly with clients, identifying possible issues that might arise and formulating strategies to address them.

Discussing Potential Risks: There may be risks associated with certain estate planning choices. For example, if a client wants to leave an uneven distribution of assets among children, it may lead to family disputes or even legal challenges. Lawyers should discuss these risks with clients and help them understand the potential consequences of their decisions.

Setting Realistic Timelines: This is essential in estate planning. Clients might expect a swift resolution, but the process often takes longer than anticipated because of the need for thoroughness and attention to detail. Lawyers should give clients a realistic estimate of how long each step will take, including drafting documents, getting them reviewed, and implementing the estate plan.

Estate planning is not a one-time event; it requires regular review and updates to reflect changes in the client's life circumstances or financial situation, or changes in the law. Lawyers should set and manage expectations for ongoing engagement, emphasizing the need for regular check-ins and potential adjustments to the estate plan over time. It's also vital that lawyers educate clients about the importance of keeping their estate plan up-to-date, communicating any significant life changes, and revisiting the plan at regular intervals.

MORE WAYS TO STAY CLIENT-FOCUSED

There are several more ways that you can keep the focus on your clients. Prompt and proactive communication is essential in a client-focused practice. Responding to clients' inquiries and providing regular updates on their case's progress demonstrate attentiveness and dedication to their legal matters.

> Prompt and proactive communication is essential in a client-focused practice.

A client-focused lawyer empowers clients by involving them in the decision-making process. Educating clients about their legal rights and options allows them to make informed choices about their cases. Adopting a client-focused approach in a legal practice also involves integrating clients' perspectives, experiences, and feedback into the core aspects of the service. This is more than just a business strategy; it is an ethical and professional commitment to excellence in legal service delivery.

Feedback can be obtained in various ways, such as through regular meetings, surveys, or informal conversations. The objective is to understand the clients' perspectives about the services received and areas where the law firm could improve. This feedback helps lawyers identify what they are doing right and what areas need improvement. It allows them to assess the effectiveness of their communication, the adequacy of the resources they have provided, and their ability to meet or exceed the clients' expectations.

Client feedback is a valuable source of information for continuous improvement. By understanding the clients' needs and expectations, lawyers can develop tailored strategies to improve service delivery. This may involve updating their communication strategies, enhancing their legal knowledge and skills, or investing in new technology to streamline processes and make legal services more accessible and efficient.

Continuous improvement also involves maintaining an updated understanding of the legal landscape and adjusting services accordingly. This means keeping abreast of changing laws and regulations, and understanding the implications of these changes for their clients. Every client interaction provides a learning opportunity for lawyers. By reflecting on these experiences, lawyers can enhance their interpersonal skills, legal expertise, and problem-solving abilities.

These lessons can help them refine their approach in handling similar situations in the future, thus improving their overall quality of service. Plus, client experiences can offer insights into market trends and emerging needs of clients, helping lawyers anticipate and prepare for future demands. This proactive approach not only improves service delivery but also fosters a sense of trust and confidence among clients.

Client-focused legal services aim to exceed clients' expectations and ensure that their experiences are positive, leading to enhanced client satisfaction and loyalty. Lawyers who commit to a client-focused approach prioritize active listening, empathy, and a thorough understanding of their clients' needs, expectations, and personal circumstances.

THINK ABOUT WHAT YOU'RE SELLING

If you want my opinion, I think there are probably only two reasons why people ever spend money. There's either something they want to acquire or achieve, or there's something they want to avoid. So whenever we're thinking about what we're selling, we need to think about what we are providing. Is it something that someone wants to acquire or something that they want to avoid?

> I think there are probably only two reasons why people ever spend money.

And by that I mean people want to avoid pain. If you can find someone's pain point and you can give them an opportunity to avoid it, then you've got something you can sell, whether that be a product or a service. And as you think about different industries and different products, you can easily identify the main thing that they are directing their marketing toward: someone's desire to acquire something or someone's avoidance of pain. But there's usually more than one issue involved with acquisition or avoidance. In any good sale of products or services, you can find multiple points of selling.

That's why when I developed MissouriTrafficTickets.com we focused on the client in two very specific ways beyond the obvious of fixing their ticket at a price they couldn't turn down.

When we started the service, we took a real hard look at "What are *all* the things that we are selling?" On the surface, we were selling a legal service: you can go online and hire a lawyer, and that lawyer will go to court or negotiate with a prosecutor for you to keep that traffic ticket off your record so that you don't get points or lose your license, or whatever. How that service played out was different in almost every case. People from all walks of life get tickets for a broad spectrum of infractions that happen in municipalities with vastly different ordinances. In a way, these cases were like snowflakes. From afar, one speeding violation looks like the next, but up close, you can see the differences.

Because of all these possible iterations, we had to think carefully about the marketing campaign for MissouriTrafficTickets.com. Primarily, I was selling a service to help people AVOID pain points like higher insurance rates or losing their driver's licenses. But it was deeper than that. Often we were helping them avoid the loss of large sums of money by getting fines reduced or eliminated. We were also doing all the work; meaning, we were also helping people avoid inconvenience.

But here are two of the unseen things we were selling: confidence and a sense of wisdom. Clients walked away from MissouriTrafficTickets.com services feeling proud to have made such a great decision in choosing our services. It gave them a sense of importance. They were so smart and crafty, avoiding huge fallouts from their traffic citations by hiring an affordable service to take care of things for them! If you've read Dale Carnegie's *How to Win Friends and Influence People* (and you should, if you haven't!) then you know how vital it is to make others feel important. The ability to empower people is another arrow in your professional sales-and-services quiver.

> It gave them a sense of importance.

The other thing we did with MissouriTrafficTickets.com that genuinely, honest-to-goodness helped people feel special, empowered, and heard is that we added what I called the "cry box." Let me take it back to my early prosecutor and criminal defense attorney days to explain where this concept came from.

One of the things that I learned fairly early on in my career is that everybody wants to tell their story. That's what sometimes makes the work of police officers and detectives so easy—people want to talk. And they'll talk. And talk. And talk. So many times, all officers need to do when they're investigating a crime is give somebody an opportunity or reason to talk, and they will tell their whole story. (And there are myriad reasons you shouldn't talk to police officers, particularly if you are innocent. But that's something for another book...)

People are so interested in telling their story that they will take any opportunity to do so. I distinctly remember one time when, as an assistant prosecuting attorney, I was preparing a witness for testimony prior to a preliminary hearing. And I specifically sat down with her, and I said, "Okay, there are some basic ground rules to testifying at a trial and being a good witness."

Then I laid out the rules:

1. Always listen to the entire question that either lawyer asks you, and then take a breath before you begin to answer. This is so you can process exactly what the question is, and if either attorney wants to object, they have the opportunity to do that. So always listen to the entire question before you start to answer.
2. ONLY answer the question you've been asked. DO NOT go into a lot of extra detail; just answer the question asked.

So I'd just given her these instructions, and I said, "Okay, we're going to practice right now. I'm going to start showing you a little bit about how I'm going to take you through your direct testimony to establish the evidence we need for this case to go forward."

She nodded that she understood, and I asked her the question.

"What day was it?"

Now, my potential witness, with whom I had just gone over the TWO VERY SPECIFIC ground rules, said, "Well, I came home that day. And when I got home, I saw a strange car in the driveway. And so that made me a little nervous to begin with. So I went to the basement door instead of the front door like I normally would, so that I could get in the house and see if there was anything different in there than what I normally expected."

Twenty minutes later, she was done telling me about the day in question. So I asked her if she even knew the question she'd been given, and she looked me straight in the eye and said, "Oh. I don't know."

Back to square one... So there are two very important ground rules...

The point is, the impulse to tell a story is so *strong* in us as humans, it's virtually irresistible.

> The point is, the impulse to tell a story is so *strong* in us as humans, it's virtually irresistible.

But in our MissouriTraffic-Tickets.com practice, all we were doing at first was helping folks keep their traffic tickets off the record. It didn't matter whether they were innocent or guilty, or what the circumstances of their actual traffic stops were. Just tell us about your ticket, pay us, and let us go help the prosecutor avoid some pain too by cutting a deal so we don't have to go to trial for someone going 5 mph over the limit in a school zone.

The system was great—for us. But remember what I said at the beginning of this chapter? The system has to work for the lawyer AND the client, and the focus should be on the client. But what we learned was that people couldn't just show us their ticket and pay us. They NEEDED to tell us their story, or else they didn't feel as if we understood them and their individual case. They weren't satisfied with the service, not because we didn't take care of their tickets but because we didn't take care of *them*.

And thus, the cry box was born; it was simply an open-ended field on the submission form where people could tell their story about their traffic stop. It said, "Please tell us whatever you think we need to know about your case in order to serve you well."

And people ate it up!

In all seriousness, we did not really care what they put in that box.

But we needed to give them the opportunity to tell their story so that they could satisfy their need to be heard. And you know what? We discovered that after we put that box in, it made our process much more efficient, because people were more likely to complete the process and go on to the sale, feeling like they'd been heard. Before the cry box, we'd dealt with a lot of phone calls to the office because people simply couldn't believe that we could resolve a ticket without every sordid detail of their traffic stop. And you know how I feel about phone calls!

What it all boils down to is that being willing to give people an outlet to tell their story is incredibly important in sales. This is particularly true if you're selling pain avoidance—people *need* to tell you about their pain. And if you can find a way for them to do that in a way that's efficient for you, like our cry box, all the better.

> Being willing to give people an outlet to tell their story is incredibly important in sales.

TYING THINGS TOGETHER

When we bind together the opportunity for people to tell their story and give feedback with the client-focused approaches of clear communication and managing expectations, we can build a rock-solid sales process. That's why it's critical to ensure that your systems are in place to serve both you and your clientele.

Of course, systems are pretty meaningless without the right people to drive them, so as we leave behind this conversation about clients, we're headed straight for a chapter about staff. Join me to discuss the best ways to find the best people to keep your practice purring like a barn cat under the milking stool.

CHAPTER 7
BUILDING YOUR SUPPORT STAFF

The success of any organization heavily relies on its support staff. Finding, hiring, and retaining the right individuals for these positions are crucial tasks that demand a comprehensive evaluation of candidates. Beyond traditional metrics like education and experience, assessing temperament, personality, and work habits becomes equally important.

Over the years, I've seen hiring methods come and go, and I have to say, the modern ability to evaluate potential employees based on more than a résumé and a handshake has been a game changer. My practice now has a lot less turnover because I have a much better understanding of how a person can fill a role *before* I hire them to fulfill it. That means that I'm spending less time and money onboarding and training new people, which puts more resources back into the business and boosts my ability to best serve my clients.

Let's take a look at some of the tools I use to assess both the needs of my practice and the strengths of my potential hires.

First, Determine Your MO

Before evaluating potential candidates, it's essential to gain insight into one's own modus operandi (MO)—how one prefers to work and get things done. Self-awareness helps identify areas where support is needed and guides the hiring process to find complementary talents. Several tools can aid in this self-assessment, and one popular choice is the Kolbe A™ Index. Full disclaimer, this test is my absolute FAVORITE professional personality-assessment tool.

> Self-awareness helps identify areas where support is needed.

The Kolbe A Index offers valuable insights by scoring individuals on four scales of MO: Fact Finder, Follow Thru, Quick Start, and Implementor. These scores range from 1 to 10, with no score being superior to another; each score represents the energy available for work in that particular area. By understanding one's own Kolbe A MO, an individual can discover their unique strengths and challenges.

Let's look at an example of a Kolbe A Index score. Here's an individual (hint: it's me!) with a Kolbe A MO of 2-3-10-3. This person has a low Fact Finder score (2), indicating that they don't require excessive details and can work effectively with minimal information. Their Follow Thru score (3) implies limited energy for reviewing and double-checking ongoing projects. The last number (3), their Implementor score, is also low, meaning they have less energy for physically building project components. However, they possess a high

Quick Start score (10), indicating a strong ability to initiate projects with enthusiasm and adaptability.

When you look to hire new employees, you want to hire people who complement you and one another. So while I discovered that I wasn't proficient in all areas—and no one is, by the way—my high Quick Start score makes me an excellent fit for roles that require quick decision-making and adaptability, such as sales, presentations, and public speaking. Law fits quite nicely into that category too. For me to succeed, I need to work with colleagues who have complementary strengths. For instance, candidates with high Fact Finder skills fill in information gaps, reducing the risk of impulsive decisions. Someone who can do that would highly complement someone like me with low Fact Finder skills but a high Quick Start score. This knowledge has been tremendously beneficial in building a support staff that thrives and helps me thrive.

Incorporating the Kolbe A Index into the hiring process enables you to assess how potential candidates' MOs fit within the existing team dynamics. Additionally, Kolbe offers a tool for score-to-score comparison, which allows individuals to understand each other's MO better. This understanding can highlight potential areas of conflict and provide insights into effective collaboration, minimizing friction among team members.

CliftonStrengths® as a Multipurpose Tool

CliftonStrengths®, developed by Gallup, is a well-respected assessment tool that unveils an individual's top five strengths from a list of thirty-four talent themes. It's an insightful tool that can serve multiple purposes as you build, train, and retain high-quality staff. The strengths assessed by Clifton-Strengths are a window into inherent abilities and passions, shedding light on what people naturally excel at. Harnessing these strengths can result in increased productivity, job satisfaction, and overall performance.

Understanding the Top Five Strengths: When you go through the CliftonStrengths assessment, it reveals your top five strengths, providing valuable insights into your core capabilities. For instance, your strengths could be "Strategic," "Relator," "Achiever," "Learner," and "Responsibility." These strengths give you a glimpse of your problem-solving skills, ability to build relationships, drive to reach your goals, passion for learning, and sense of ownership.

> Harnessing these strengths can result in increased productivity, job satisfaction, and overall performance.

Optimizing Roles and Responsibilities: By recognizing each individual's unique combination of strengths, employers can tailor roles and responsibilities for their support staff. Matching tasks with an individual's strengths boosts their engagement and motivation, leading to higher job satisfaction and productivity. For instance, if someone excels in "Strategic" thinking, they might shine in roles that involve analyzing complex situations and coming up with innovative solutions.

Building Complementary Teams: A diverse support staff boasting a wide range of strengths is crucial for a well-rounded team. CliftonStrengths not only identifies individual strengths but also highlights complementary ones that can create synergy within the team. Consider pairing someone strong in "Relator" skills with another who excels in "Communication"—this dynamic duo can foster effective collaboration and provide exceptional customer service.

Retaining Talent Through Strengths Development: Hiring the right people is just the beginning; retaining them is equally vital. Organizations can nurture professional growth and job satisfaction by investing in the development of strengths. Regular coaching and training sessions help employees harness their strengths and apply them effectively in their roles.

Team Building and Collaboration: CliftonStrengths can also serve as a powerful tool for team building. Organizing group workshops where team members share their strengths promotes mutual understanding and appreciation. Recognizing and valuing each other's strengths enhances cooperation and teamwork, resulting in a more harmonious and productive work environment.

The CliftonStrengths assessment tool offers profound insights into the natural talents and strengths of potential support staff members. By leveraging this understanding, organizations can fine-tune roles, assemble complementary teams, and cultivate a positive workplace atmosphere. When employees have opportunities to showcase their strengths, job satisfaction and productivity skyrocket, leading to a highly successful support staff. By embracing CliftonStrengths and prioritizing strengths development, organizations can unlock the full potential of their team, ensuring sustained growth and success.

Good Ol' Myers-Briggs

The Myers-Briggs Type Indicator® (MBTI®), rooted in Carl Jung's personality theory, assesses individuals across four pairs of traits: Extraversion (E)—Introversion (I); Sensing (S)—Intuition (N); Thinking (T)—Feeling (F); and Judging (J)—Perceiving (P). It neatly categorizes people into one of sixteen personality types based on their preferences. The Myers-Briggs assessment is a classic personality assessment that many people are familiar with, and most professionals have taken it at least once in their careers.

> The Myers-Briggs assessment is a classic personality assessment that many people are familiar with.

The MBTI provides valuable insights into how individuals perceive and interact with their world. For example, someone might be an "ISTJ"—Introverted, Sensing, Thinking, and Judging—indicating a preference for structured work environments, data analysis, and logical problem-solving. Understanding the MBTI types of support staff members is the key to assembling a harmonious, diverse team. Different personality types bring unique qualities to the table, enriching decision-making and problem-solving. Imagine a team with a mix of "INTJ"s (Introverted, Intuitive, Thinking, and Judging) and "ENFP"s (Extraverted, Intuitive, Feeling, and Perceiving) benefiting from INTJs' strategic thinking and ENFPs' creativity and interpersonal skills.

MBTI insights can also significantly improve communication among team members. Knowing each individual's communication style allows for more effective interactions, as team members can tailor their approach to suit the preferences of others. Furthermore, understanding potential areas of conflict based on personality differences enables proactive resolution and fosters a harmonious work environment.

When employers consider MBTI types while assigning roles and responsibilities, they ensure a better fit between staff members and their tasks. For instance, individuals with a "Feeling" preference might shine in customer-facing roles, bringing empathy and understanding to interactions, while those with a "Thinking" preference could excel in analytical and strategic roles.

MBTI also promotes personal and professional development. Understanding one's personality type allows individuals to identify their strengths and weaknesses and seek opportunities for growth. Employers can offer targeted training and coaching to help support staff optimize their performance.

The Myers-Briggs Type Indicator is a potent tool for recognizing personality preferences and nurturing an inclusive and productive support team. By harnessing MBTI insights during the hiring process, employers can build a diverse team of individuals whose strengths complement one another. Additionally, comprehending MBTI types within the team facilitates effective communication, conflict resolution, and role allocation. Embracing MBTI not only enhances team dynamics but also encourages personal and professional growth, culminating in a highly successful support staff and a thriving organization.

Tools to Improve Employee Retention

Using tools like Kolbe A, CliftonStrengths, and Myers-Briggs during the hiring process and to foster a supportive team environment can significantly contribute to employee retention. Here's how:

Job Satisfaction: When employees are placed in roles that align with their natural strengths and preferences, they tend to enjoy their work more, reducing the likelihood of seeking opportunities elsewhere.

Personal Growth and Development: Offering targeted training and coaching based on individual strengths and personality types enhances skills and demonstrates the organization's commitment to growth, increasing loyalty and a sense of belonging.

Improved Team Dynamics: Understanding personality differences and preferences within the team helps minimize conflicts and promotes better collaboration, enhancing employee engagement and commitment.

Effective Communication: Awareness of each other's communication styles allows team members to adapt their approach for clearer, more efficient interactions, fostering a positive work atmosphere.

Empowerment and Autonomy: Leveraging employees' strengths empowers them to take ownership of tasks they excel in, boosting confidence and job satisfaction, and making them more likely to stay.

Recognition and Appreciation: Understanding individual strengths and personality types enables managers to recognize and appreciate employees for their unique contributions, strengthening the bond between the employee and the organization.

Career Paths and Alignment: By identifying employees' strengths and aspirations, organizations can align their career paths with available opportunities, reducing the desire to seek advancement elsewhere.

Work-Life Balance: Understanding personality preferences aids in creating a work environment that accommodates individual needs and preferences, leading to improved work-life balance.

Sense of Purpose: Aligning employees' roles with their strengths and values fosters a sense of purpose in their work, increasing dedication to the organization.

Employee Engagement: Engaged employees who feel connected with their work and colleagues are less likely to seek opportunities elsewhere. Understanding their strengths and providing resources and support enhances engagement levels.

Incorporating tools like Kolbe A, CliftonStrengths, and Myers-Briggs in the hiring process and nurturing a supportive work environment based on individual strengths and preferences can significantly impact employee retention. When employees feel valued and empowered, and have growth opportunities, they are more likely to stay committed to the organization, reducing turnover and fostering a strong and cohesive support team.

> When employees feel valued and empowered, and have growth opportunities, they are more likely to stay committed to the organization.

Speaking of Value

Now, I won't profess to know anything about your practice's finances, so I can't tell you how to structure your pay scale. What I can tell you is what works for me, and then you can form your own opinion on it. Ready?

I don't pay my employees an hourly wage or a set salary. True story.

All my employees are paid based on our gross revenues. They get a straight cut—a percentage of the gross. If I have a bad month, they have a bad month. I have found this arrangement to be extremely effective in various ways. For us, a profit-sharing full commission model of employee compensation offers several advantages over traditional wages or salary systems. Here are some key reasons it works for us.

Motivation and Performance:

- In a profit-sharing full-commission model, employees directly benefit from the company's success.

- This creates strong incentives for them to perform at their best and contribute to the organization's growth.
- Direct impact on earnings leads to higher motivation, proactivity, and commitment to achieving outstanding results.

Alignment of Interests:

- Unlike fixed wages or salaries, this model aligns employees' interests with those of the company.
- A financial stake in the organization's success encourages actions and decisions for long-term benefit.

Cost Control:

- From the employer's perspective, this model offers cost-control advantages.
- Compensation is linked to revenue or profitability, resulting in commissions paid only when supported by actual revenue.
- This helps manage labor costs during slower periods and provides compensation-expense flexibility.

Merit-Based Compensation:

- The model rewards employees based on individual performance and contributions to the bottom line.
- It also attracts and retains high-performing individuals who excel in a competitive environment.

Entrepreneurial Mindset:

- The arrangement fosters an entrepreneurial mindset among employees.
- It encourages thinking like business owners and actively seeking opportunities for sales and profitability growth.

Flexibility in Earning Potential:

- The model offers employees more control over their earning potential compared to fixed wages or salaries.
- High-performing individuals can achieve significant financial rewards, enhancing job satisfaction and loyalty.

Focus on Customer Satisfaction:

- Employees recognize that their income depends on customer satisfaction and repeat business.
- This drives exceptional customer service and fosters long-term client relationships.

Retention of Top Talent:

- The model attracts and retains top talent, particularly sales-oriented and self-motivated individuals.
- It also rewards hard work and success directly, making it an appealing compensation structure.

Atmosphere of Fairness:

- The arrangement is perceived as more fair and transparent since compensation is tied to measurable performance metrics.
- This fosters a culture of meritocracy, where employees believe their efforts are justly rewarded.

Continuous Improvement:

- The commission structure encourages continuous improvement and learning.
- It motivates employees to seek professional-development opportunities and enhance their skills to maximize earning potential.

Again, this is something that works very well for us, and it's food for thought for your practice too.

Final Thoughts on Staffing

For my practice, using personality assessments, crafting dream teams, and shaking up compensation systems isn't just a smart move—it's a game changer. Tools like Kolbe A, CliftonStrengths, and Myers-Briggs are like secret weapons that help organizations understand their support staff on a whole new level. These assessments don't just tell you about people; they bring them together. Imagine a team where everyone's quirks and strengths fit together like puzzle pieces. That's what

> Imagine a team where everyone's quirks and strengths fit together like puzzle pieces.

you get when you use these tools. It's like turning a group of individuals into a well-oiled machine.

And let's not forget about compensation systems, like the profit-sharing full commission model. It's more than just a paycheck; it's a motivator. When your paycheck is directly linked to the company's success, you've got skin in the game. It's like saying, "Hey, your hard work matters, and it's going to pay off." This approach attracts the go-getters—the folks who love a challenge. They start thinking like entrepreneurs, always looking for ways to make things better. And the best part? They're happier and more loyal, and they stick around.

So, what's the result of all this? Well, it's a workplace where people love what they do—where they work together like a well-tuned orchestra. It's an organization that's ready to take on anything the future throws at it. It's not just about the bottom line; it's about creating a workplace where everyone thrives and the whole team wins.

Now that we've gone through building systems and building staff, let's talk about building clientele. In the next chapter, we'll take a look at seminars: what they really are, what they really do, and how you can leverage a well-put-together seminar into a surge in new clients.

CHAPTER 8

INTRODUCTION TO SEMINARS

Ask anyone, and they'll tell you that the tried-and-true method of gaining estate planning clients on your own is free seminars. If you want to build a practice, mastering the seminar is essential.

There are several keys to why seminars work so well. First of all, they can be low-overhead affairs. There are usually local community rooms available at libraries or other public buildings that can be reserved for little to no money. While many presenters offer a meal, including up to a free steak dinner, I never have. It's always felt gimmicky, and I want people there who want an estate plan—not people who just want a free steak. The free-meal hook isn't necessary. With a good presentation and good marketing, you can fill a room.

> If you want to build a practice, mastering the seminar is essential.

To be frank with you, ten people is about the smallest crowd I'm comfortable with; any fewer and the room feels empty and lacks energy. On the other end of the spectrum, the largest crowd I've spoken to is about one hundred people. Any more than that, and I'm not able to form a personal connection. The personal connection is essential to your listeners. In the last section of this book, we're going to talk you through perfecting your seminar content, but first, let's finish discussing why seminars are the perfect vehicle for attracting new clients and the skills you'll need to prepare to launch your first seminar.

TIME TO DO SOME MATH!

Once your seminar marketing is fine-tuned, you should be able to attract attendees to your seminar for an average cost of around $300 per person (or what I like to call a "buying unit"). A buying unit can represent either an individual or a couple.

For instance, if you have a room that can accommodate twenty people, that's roughly ten to fifteen buying units. So the cost to bring these people to your seminar would amount to approximately $3,000–$4,500, not including expenses for the venue, refreshments, handouts, marketing materials, and so on. It's a good idea to plan your budget for each seminar for around $5,000–$6,000. The next crucial factor to consider is your presentation skills. How effectively can you convert seminar attendees into appointments in your conference room?

If you have ten to fifteen buying units in a seminar, and five to eight of them set an appointment with you, you've converted 50 percent of attendees into potential clients. Now, if they all keep their consultation appointments with you and two to four of those buying units decide to go ahead with your estate planning services, you've once again converted at 50 percent. Congratulations! Depending on your fees, you've just gained $4,000–$16,000 from clients who attended your seminar.

What if you could do better? After five years of refining and perfecting my seminars, my average on-the-spot, post-seminar appointment-setting percentage is just over 90 percent. Of those appointments, I convert 90 percent again into new clients. Based on the average size of my seminar audience, I can generally count on eight to twelve new cases per seminar, or $16,000–$48,000 in gross sales each time.

> What if you could do better?

And if I can get a big room, that just scales up. That's the beauty of it.

As seminars grow in size, it may become necessary to train other members of the firm to deliver presentations. This approach not only helps distribute the workload but also injects different perspectives and presentation styles into the seminars, potentially attracting diverse audience segments.

The advantages of scaling seminar marketing efforts are numerous:

> *Reaching New Markets*: Scaling seminars allows estate planners to tap into new market segments, including different geographical areas, demographic groups, or industry sectors. This diversification can lead to a more varied client base and create fresh avenues for growth.
>
> *Enhanced Brand Recognition*: Larger seminars and more extensive marketing initiatives can significantly

boost the firm's brand recognition. The greater the number of people who are aware of and understand the firm's services, the higher the potential for attracting new clients.

Increased Consultations and Conversions: With increased brand recognition and a broader audience, estate planners may witness a rise in consultations and, subsequently, client conversions. This can translate into increased revenue and overall business growth.

Sustainable Growth: Implementing scalable solutions empowers financial professionals to reach a larger pool of potential clients. This contributes to sustained growth and long-term success.

You can gauge the effectiveness of seminars by meticulously tracking conversion rates. This involves monitoring the progression of seminar attendees to appointments and, ultimately, to estate planning cases. By doing this, you can calculate the average gross sales generated per seminar. This data serves as a valuable tool for making strategic adjustments and improvements to maximize return on investment (ROI).

Continuous refinement and improvement of seminars are critical factors for boosting conversion rates. The initial step in refining seminars is collecting and analyzing feedback from attendees. This feedback offers insights into what worked, what didn't, and areas that require improvement. Encourage attendees to provide honest feedback through surveys or feedback forms. This valuable input can help identify potential adjustments in content, presentation style, duration, or interaction methods.

A/B testing, a user-experience research methodology, can also be an effective way to refine seminars. This involves making one change at a time (such as a different call to action [CTA], a change in the presentation style, or a different seminar duration) and comparing the results to the original format. This can help identify what changes lead to higher conversion rates.

An appointment-setting rate above 90 percent and a subsequent closure rate of a little over 90 percent are remarkable achievements, and I'm very proud of them. These figures demonstrate that the seminars not only attract potential clients but also effectively drive them to commit to estate planning services. And, after all, that's the crux of a seminar—introducing people to your product, which you've carefully cultivated to help people get the most out of their estate planning.

Let's Get Personal

I talk a lot about creating a personal connection during a seminar, and this goes beyond merely delivering information. It requires the art of rapport-building, empathy, and active engagement. Here are several strategies that financial professionals can employ to forge these connections during their presentations:

> It requires the art of rapport-building, empathy, and active engagement.

Relatable Communication: Simplify complex estate planning information using everyday language instead of industry jargon. Share real-life examples and anecdotes that resonate with the audience, bridging the gap between the presenter and attendees.

Personalization: Injecting personal stories or experiences related to estate planning can humanize the presenter and make them more approachable. Addressing attendees by their names during the seminar or while providing examples can also foster familiarity and rapport.

Active Listening: Actively listening to attendees' questions and concerns is paramount. Acknowledge their input and respond thoughtfully. Expressing empathy by understanding and sharing their feelings leaves a lasting impression. When attendees share personal stories or concerns, offer understanding and supportive feedback.

Audience Participation: Encourage engagement through interactive elements like polls, quizzes, or breakout discussions. A two-way dialogue, rather than a one-way presentation, can make attendees feel more connected and involved.

The more connected you can make an audience feel, the more likely they are to trust you to provide them with exceptional service, so get out there and get personal!

Build Your Skills for Seminar Success

Effective and impactful seminars hinge on polished presentation skills. The ability to communicate clearly and confidently can significantly boost audience engagement and foster a better understanding of the material. Let's delve into why each of these aspects matters.

Clear Articulation: Presenters should articulate their points in an easily understandable manner, avoiding excessive technical jargon. Simplicity and clarity can be the difference between an engaged audience and a confused one. Practicing pronunciation and articulation is particularly beneficial for those who naturally speak quickly or softly.

Nonverbal Cues: Positive body language, such as maintaining eye contact, using open gestures, and facing the audience, builds trust and rapport. Conversely, negative body language, like crossed arms or lack of eye contact, creates a barrier.

Pace Variability: The speed of delivery matters. Speaking too fast can confuse, while speaking too slowly can bore. Striking a balance and varying the pace throughout the presentation maintains attention and interest.

Voice Modulation: A monotone voice can disengage the audience. Changing tone, volume, and speed makes the presentation dynamic and engaging. Emphasizing key points through voice modulation enhances understanding.

Effective Visual Aids: Visual aids, such as slides or props, enhance comprehension and provide variety. They should complement the speech, not distract from it.

Here are some other ways you can effectively connect with an audience to broaden their understanding of your services and make them more likely to convert from attendees into clients.

Invest in Training: Professional training or hiring a presentation coach can significantly improve skills. Personalized feedback and techniques enhance clarity, body language, pace, voice modulation, and the use of visual aids.

Rehearse: Multiple rehearsals familiarize presenters with content, identify potential issues, and boost confidence. Ideally, rehearsals should mimic the actual presentation setting.

Update Your Content: Content should be continually updated and refined to keep seminars engaging and valuable. This might involve including recent legal changes, incorporating real-life examples, or presenting information in a more engaging manner.

Don't Avoid Personalization: Providing personalized experiences enhances connections with attendees. This can involve tailoring content to specific audience needs or adjusting follow-up communication based on questions or feedback.

Provide an Effective CTA: A compelling CTA is vital for converting attendees into clients. It should clearly and persuasively communicate the next steps, whether that's scheduling a consultation, downloading a resource, or attending another seminar.

Experimentation with different CTAs can help find what resonates best with the audience.

The more you can do, the more you should do. You want your seminars to be fun, informative, and, most of all, lucrative!

Here! Have Some More Marketing Ideas

Seminars, done right, will become your number one marketing tool, but they don't have to be your only marketing tool! Partnering with other organizations or experts can be a highly effective strategy to broaden your reach. These partnerships can include financial advisers, insurance companies, elder-care facilities, community centers, or even other law firms not specializing in estate planning. Collaborations enable estate planners to provide attendees with more comprehensive knowledge and tap into the established audiences of their partners.

> Seminars, done right, will become your number one marketing tool.

You can also consider going online with your presentations. The advent of digital technology has revolutionized seminar marketing efforts. Webinars and online seminars have emerged as powerful tools, allowing estate planning professionals to reach geographically dispersed audiences. They are cost-effective and easier to organize, enabling frequent events and significantly larger audiences. Estate planners can further expand their reach by seeking public-speaking opportunities at conferences, business meetings, or community events. These platforms offer access to larger and more diverse audience groups and enhance estate planners' reputation as experts in the field.

Mastering the art of seminar marketing for estate planning demands dedication, preparation, and a deep understanding of client needs. By harnessing personal connections and continuously improving seminar presentations, you can establish yourself as a trusted industry adviser. Additionally, the ability to convert seminar attendees into loyal estate planning clients fuels sustainable growth and revenue increase.

Perfecting seminar marketing is not just a testament to professional growth but also an investment in building a thriving estate planning practice. When you embrace the potential of seminars, you unlock a potent marketing strategy, opening doors to new opportunities and cementing leadership in the estate planning field. Tune in to the following chapters to discover how you can take all your newfound knowledge about seminars and craft the perfect presentation to help you grow your estate planning practice!

CHAPTER 9

WHEN GOOD SEMINARS GO BAD

In the last chapter, we talked about the role that seminars can play in growing and sustaining your estate planning practice. In this chapter, we're going to dive a little deeper into some of the tips, tricks, obstacles, and fine-tuning of seminar presenting. We certainly don't want you to end up on the next episode of (*dramatic announcer voice*) *When Good Seminars Go Bad.* Of course, that's not a real show, but if it were, trust me, you would not want to be featured!

Presenting a seminar isn't an easy task; it takes preparation and practice to get things right. Let's reinforce some of the basics you learned in Chapter 8 and look at some of the challenges in and solutions to delivering effective, well-received seminars.

> Presenting a seminar isn't an easy task.

Understanding Pitfalls

Estate planning seminars can be powerful tools for engaging with potential clients, showcasing both professionals' expertise and building trust. However, not all seminars deliver the desired outcomes. In some cases, these events can go awry and fail to connect with the audience. Understanding the common pitfalls that lead to ineffective seminars is crucial to avoid costly mistakes and create impactful presentations. It's time to look at some challenges and solutions to ensure that your seminars aren't wasting your or anyone else's time.

Using the Power of Personalization

One significant reason estate planning seminars often miss the mark is a lack of personalization. A one-size-fits-all approach may not resonate with attendees, who come with diverse financial goals and concerns. Successful estate planning seminars go the extra mile. They invest time in researching and truly understanding the needs and preferences of their audience. Tailoring the content to address attendees' specific concerns and challenges demonstrates genuine care and consideration for their unique circumstances. This personalized approach not only boosts audience engagement but also builds trust, establishing you as a reliable and empathetic adviser. Here are some strategies for personalization:

> *Conduct Audience Research*: Before the seminar, gather information about the demographic and financial profiles of the attendees. Use questionnaires and surveys to understand their concerns, goals, and existing estate planning knowledge. This research helps

you tailor the presentation to resonate with the audience and address their unique interests.

Identify Common Concerns: Analyze the collected data to identify recurring concerns and pain points among the audience. Whether it's ensuring their children's financial security or minimizing tax implications, pinpointing these recurring themes enables you to focus on the most relevant topics during the seminar.

Address Real-Life Scenarios: Incorporate real-life scenarios that mirror the experiences of your audience. Share case studies or anecdotes that reflect the challenges faced by attendees. By presenting relatable situations, you illustrate how proper estate planning can address these issues and provide solutions.

Customize Content: Adjust the depth and complexity of the presentation to match the audience's level of understanding. Avoid overwhelming novices with technical jargon, while ensuring that those with more advanced knowledge find value in the content. Striking the right balance ensures that all attendees feel included and engaged.

Offer Tailored Solutions: Suggest specific estate planning solutions based on the audience's needs. Whether it's recommending trusts for blended families or outlining strategies for charitable giving, offering tailored solutions showcases your expertise and demonstrates that you understand their unique circumstances.

Follow Up Personally: After the seminar, reach out to attendees individually to address any remaining concerns. Offer one-on-one consultations or follow-up meetings to discuss their specific estate planning needs further. This personalized attention reinforces your commitment to their financial well-being.

By tailoring your estate planning seminar to address the specific concerns and preferences of your audience, you elevate the presentation to a new level of success. With a personalized approach, you establish yourself as a caring and trustworthy professional, dedicated to guiding your audience through their estate planning journey with expertise and empathy.

No "Amateur Hour" Delivery, Please!

Effective estate planning seminars not only require well-structured content but also the ability to connect emotionally with the audience. Presenters must master various aspects of communication, including tone, body language, and pace, to ensure an engaging and impactful delivery.

> Presenters must master various aspects of communication.

Address the Emotional Dimension: Estate planning is a topic laden with emotional significance. Focusing solely on technical aspects without acknowledging the emotional aspect may lead to a disconnection from the audience.

Empathetic Engagement: Begin by empathizing with the attendees, recognizing the profound impact estate planning decisions can have on their lives and loved ones. Express understanding for the emotional complexities involved.

Provoke Reflection: Encourage attendees to contemplate their own fears, hopes, and aspirations regarding estate planning. Thoughtful questions prompt participants to reflect on their family's future, legacy, and the emotional impact of their decisions.

Create a Supportive Atmosphere: Ensure attendees feel safe and supported during the seminar. Emphasize that discussions about emotions and finances are encouraged and are confidential. This environment fosters open sharing of thoughts and feelings.

Don't Ignore Common Concerns: Discuss prevalent fears and concerns linked to estate planning, such as asset protection, providing for loved ones, and ensuring a smooth wealth transfer. Show how proper estate planning can alleviate these worries.

Celebrate Aspirations: Highlight the positive aspects of estate planning, including the fulfillment of personal aspirations and charitable goals. Share stories of individuals who left a lasting impact on their communities through proper planning.

By recognizing and addressing the emotional dimension of estate planning decisions, you infuse your presentation with empathy and relatability. This creates a safe and supportive environment for attendees to share their personal stories and financial concerns, fostering trust and deeper connections.

Ultimately, an empathetic and relatable presentation empowers individuals to make well-informed and emotionally fulfilling estate planning decisions aligned with their values and aspirations.

WATCH YOUR LANGUAGE!

No, I don't mean profanity. I mean jargon. Estate planning seminars often run into trouble when they bombard attendees with excessive technical jargon. In these presentations, offering clarity and avoiding overwhelming complexity are essential for effectively connecting with your audience. To truly engage your audience and empower them to make informed decisions about their estate plans, consider the following strategies for simplifying the material:

> *Use Plain Language*: Opt for straightforward, everyday language when explaining estate planning concepts. Avoid legal jargon and technical terms that may befuddle nonprofessionals. Instead, use relatable language that resonates with everyone, regardless of their financial knowledge.

> *Break Down Complex Ideas*: Tackle intricate concepts in manageable, bite-sized pieces. Present information step by step, offering clear explanations for each facet of estate planning. This approach helps attendees process the information gradually and prevents them from feeling overwhelmed.

> *Use Visual Aids and Infographics*: Enhance understanding with visual aids and infographics. These visual representations can simplify complex ideas and make

information more accessible. Think of flow charts, diagrams, or graphs to illustrate key points and relationships between different estate planning elements.

Provide Analogies and Real-Life Examples: Contextualize complex concepts by using analogies and real-life scenarios. Analogies make abstract ideas more tangible and relatable. Relate estate planning concepts to familiar situations or objects that the audience can easily grasp. Real-life examples can also illustrate how estate planning impacts everyday life.

Encourage Questions and Interaction: Create an open and welcoming environment that invites audience members to ask questions and seek clarification during the presentation. This two-way interaction fosters engagement and ensures that the audience stays connected to the material.

Focus on Key Takeaways: Highlight the most crucial points and actions that attendees should remember. Summarize key takeaways at the end of each section to reinforce the main concepts. Emphasize the importance of essential estate planning elements, such as wills, trusts, and beneficiary designations.

Avoid Overloading with Information: Resist the urge to include every minute detail in your presentation. While comprehensive information is valuable, overwhelming the audience with excessive details can lead to disengagement. Focus on the most pertinent and impactful information to keep the presentation clear and concise.

In your estate planning presentation, finding the equilibrium between clarity and complexity is critical to establishing a meaningful connection with your audience. This personalized and simplified approach solidifies your position as a trusted adviser genuinely concerned about your audience's understanding and financial well-being.

Don't Let Boredom Creep In

When it's a professional presenting solo the whole time, a seminar can come across as monotonous. To breathe life into an estate planning seminar, incorporate interactive elements to make it dynamic and captivating for your attendees. Engaging the audience through group discussions and case studies fosters active participation and establishes a stronger connection between the presenter and the audience.

Here's how to effectively infuse interactive elements into your seminar:

> When it's a professional presenting solo the whole time, a seminar can come across as monotonous.

Group Discussions: Divide the audience into small groups to deliberate on particular estate planning scenarios. Pose thought-provoking questions or present case studies to ignite discussions. Permit each group to share their insights, creating a collaborative learning environment.

Polling and Surveys: Incorporate live polling or anonymous surveys to collect audience feedback. Pose multiple-choice questions about estate planning preferences or common misconceptions. Display the results to stimulate further discussion and highlight pertinent topics. There are some great free smartphone apps you can use to conduct this type of polling.

Role-Playing Exercises: Engage the audience with role-playing exercises that exemplify estate planning situations. Assign participants different roles, such as beneficiaries, executors, or estate planners. These exercises provide hands-on insight into how various decisions impact the estate planning process.

Case Studies: Share real-life case studies that illustrate the significance of estate planning. Analyze scenarios where effective estate planning played a pivotal role in safeguarding assets or preserving family harmony. Discuss the outcomes and the lessons applicable to the attendees' own situations.

Interactive Worksheets: Distribute interactive worksheets that guide attendees through crucial estate planning considerations. These worksheets help participants organize their thoughts and identify key areas of focus for their estate plans. This hands-on approach makes the concepts more tangible and applicable.

Audience Polling for Topics: Empower the audience by allowing them to select which topics they'd like to explore further. Before the seminar or during a break, present a list of potential topics or areas of interest. Permit the audience to vote for their preferences, then adapt the presentation accordingly to address their priorities.

By incorporating interactive elements like group discussions and case studies, your estate planning seminar can transform into an engaging and participatory experience. These interactive exercises encourage attendees to actively apply the concepts to their own lives and equip them with tools to make informed decisions about their financial futures and their loved ones' well-being.

SET CLEAR, REALISTIC EXPECTATIONS

In the world of estate planning seminars, the road to success starts with honest and transparent marketing practices. Nothing can deter attendees more than a mismatch between their expectations and the actual content of the seminar. To ensure that your event lives up to its promises and leaves attendees satisfied, it's crucial to have clear messaging and marketing. This not only builds trust but also sets the stage for a receptive audience with an open mindset. Here's how to ensure your seminar marketing is both clear and honest:

> It's crucial to have clear messaging and marketing.

Clearly Define the Seminar's Purpose: In all your promotional materials, make it crystal clear what the seminar is about. Whether it's an introduction to estate planning concepts, an in-depth exploration of strategies, or specialized topics like wills and trusts, attendees should know exactly what to expect from the event.

Outline the Topics Covered: Provide a detailed agenda listing the key topics and concepts to be discussed during the seminar. By breaking down the content into specific sections and including brief descriptions, attendees can better understand how the material aligns with their needs and interests.

Clarify the Audience's Benefits: Explain the practical value attendees will gain from participating. Whether it's insights into effective estate planning techniques, knowledge about potential tax-saving strategies, or an understanding of asset protection, highlight the real-world advantages they'll receive.

Set Realistic Expectations: Be upfront about the level of detail and complexity covered in the seminar. Avoid any tendency to over-promise or exaggerate the content. Clearly communicate whether the seminar is introductory, intermediate, or advanced, so attendees know what to expect.

Promote Interactive Elements: If your seminar includes interactive components like group discussions or case studies, mention these in your marketing materials. This not only encourages active participation but also prepares attendees for an engaging experience.

Disclose Seminar Fees and Costs Upfront: Clearly state any associated fees for the seminar or any special offers. Whether there's a registration fee or an optional service provided at an additional cost, disclose all relevant financial information upfront. This transparency builds trust and ensures there are no surprises on the day of the event.

Provide Testimonials and Reviews: To showcase the seminar's value, include testimonials from previous attendees. Sharing positive feedback from past participants adds credibility to your event and reinforces the benefits that attendees can expect.

Transparent and honest marketing practices are the foundation of a successful estate planning seminar. This transparency ensures that attendees know what they're signing up for, making them more engaged and satisfied with the event. Ultimately, by managing expectations effectively, you create a seminar experience that aligns with the needs and interests of your audience, leaving them better informed and empowered to make sound estate planning decisions.

Managing Disruptive Audience Members

While it is extremely unlikely that you'll need to do so, handling unruly or disruptive individuals during a seminar is a challenge that requires professionalism and tact. Here are strategies for effectively managing such situations:

Maintain Composure: As a presenter, it's crucial to stay calm and composed when faced with disruptive behavior. Avoid reacting emotionally and set a positive example of professionalism for the rest of the audience.

Acknowledge and Listen: Recognize the disruptive individual and actively listen to their concerns. Show respect for their viewpoint, allowing them to express their thoughts. This demonstrates your willingness to listen and can help de-escalate the situation.

Stay Neutral and Objective: Respond to disruptive behavior with neutrality and objectivity. Avoid taking the disruption personally or engaging in confrontations. Keep your responses courteous and professional, focusing on the seminar's subject matter.

Redirect the Focus: Gently guide the conversation back to the seminar's topic and objectives. Explain that the presentation covers specific estate planning principles and offer to address individual concerns during Q&A sessions or after the presentation.

Set Boundaries: Establish clear boundaries for appropriate behavior at the beginning of the seminar. Remind the audience of the seminar's guidelines and the importance of respecting others' time and the flow of the presentation.

Seek Support: If necessary, enlist assistance from event organizers or colleagues to address disruptive behavior. In some cases, intervention from others can help manage the situation effectively.

Private Discussion: If disruptions persist, offer to speak with the disruptive individual privately after the seminar. Addressing their concerns one-on-one may lead to a more constructive resolution.

> *Focus on the Majority:* Ensure your attention remains on the engaged and respectful majority of the audience. Don't allow one disruptive individual to dominate the presentation; continue engaging with those eager to learn and participate.

Handling disruptive audience members demands poise, patience, and professionalism. By staying composed, actively listening, and refocusing on the seminar's objectives, you can effectively manage these situations. Remember that the majority of the audience is there to learn, and your focus should remain on providing them with a positive and informative seminar.

Key Takeaways About Challenges and Solutions

When it comes to estate planning, the value of seminars extends far beyond traditional presentations. These events have the potential to become dynamic and immersive experiences, fostering deeper connections and understanding among attendees. As we conclude our journey into the art of estate planning seminars, let's recap the key takeaways and the impact of personalized, simplified, and interactive approaches.

> *Personalization:* Successful seminars go beyond one-size-fits-all strategies, acknowledging the diverse financial goals and concerns of their audience. By tailoring content to address specific attendee needs, estate planning professionals demonstrate genuine care and consideration for individual circumstances. This personalized approach not only boosts audience

engagement but also builds trust, establishing financial professionals as reliable and empathetic advisers.

Simplification: Estate planning can be a complex subject, but striking the right balance between clarity and complexity is essential. Simplifying technical jargon and presenting information in clear terms ensures that every attendee can grasp the material. By making estate planning accessible to all, professionals empower their audience to make informed decisions and feel confident about their financial futures.

Interaction: Transforming seminars from unidirectional lectures to interactive experiences breathes life into the content. Engaging the audience strengthens the connection between presenters and attendees. This interaction not only keeps the audience engaged but also allows them to actively apply the concepts discussed to their unique situations, leaving them better prepared for their estate planning journey.

Estate planning seminars, when approached with personalization, simplification, and interaction in mind, become powerful tools for financial professionals. These events empower attendees to make informed decisions about their financial futures and their loved ones' well-being. In fostering meaningful connections and promoting understanding, estate planning seminars exemplify the true essence of financial advisory: guiding individuals toward brighter and more secure futures.

Now that you're armed with these solutions, let's dive even deeper into the nitty-gritty. In the next chapter, I'll share with you all the secrets to writing and delivering presentations that will knock the audience's socks off. See you on the next page.

CHAPTER 10

THE SUCCESSFUL SPEECH

We ought to call this chapter "Make It Happen," because that's what it's all about. From preparation through presentation, here's where you'll find all the nitty-gritty on delivering a seminar your attendees won't soon forget. We've got *a lot* of ground to cover, so let's get moving.

MAKE IT POLISHED

Before you can deliver a speech, seminar, or presentation, you've got to write it and practice it. Here are some tips for outlining and assembling a presentation that will wow the crowd. And remember, you don't have to reinvent the wheel! There are amazing resources and graphics out there for you to draw from—no need to make those from scratch!

> *Create an Outline*: Organize your speech with a clear outline, highlighting essential topics you wish to cover. Structure your presentation to gradually build on

foundational concepts, moving toward more intricate aspects of estate planning. This way, you cater to both novices and those who seek more advanced insights.

Use Slides: Enhance your speech with visually appealing slides that complement your presentation and reinforce key points. Visual aids can significantly enhance the impact of your estate planning presentation. When used thoughtfully, they can clarify complex concepts, reinforce key points, and maintain audience engagement.

Focus on Impactful Images: Select images that are relevant and meaningful, and that reinforce the central themes of your speech. High-quality visuals, such as photographs or graphics, can evoke emotions and create a lasting impression. For instance, an image of a happy family or a secure home can emphasize the significance of estate planning in protecting loved ones and assets.

Use Concise Bullet Points: Use bullet points sparingly to highlight key ideas or action steps. Bullet points are an effective way to break down complex information into bite-sized pieces, aiding understanding and retention. Limit each slide to a few concise points to maintain clarity and focus.

Limit Text on Slides: Avoid overcrowding slides with lengthy paragraphs or excessive text. The purpose of visual aids is to complement your spoken words, not to replicate them. Keep text to a minimum, using it only to reinforce critical points or provide key takeaways.

This encourages your audience to listen to you actively rather than reading from the slides.

Incorporate Visuals as Storytelling Tools: Use visuals to tell a story and create a narrative that resonates with your audience. Instead of relying solely on text to convey information, craft a visual journey that unfolds throughout your presentation. This approach captivates your audience and keeps them engaged with the evolving storyline.

Maintain a Consistent Design: Maintain a cohesive design throughout your visual aids to ensure a professional and polished appearance. Use a consistent color scheme, fonts, and formatting to unify your slides. This not only enhances the visual appeal but also makes it easier for your audience to follow along seamlessly.

Balance Visuals with Spoken Explanations: Avoid relying solely on visuals to convey information; supplement them with verbal explanations. While images and bullet points can be powerful aids, they should complement your speech rather than replace it. Be sure to elaborate on the visuals, providing context and further insights to enhance understanding.

> Avoid relying solely on visuals to convey information.

Practice Delivery and Tone: Rehearse your presentation to perfect your delivery and fine-tune your tone. Pay attention to the pitch, volume, and modulation of your voice. Aim for a warm and friendly tone that is approachable and fosters a comfortable atmosphere for attendees.

Maintain Positive Body Language: Be mindful of your body language during the seminar. Stand tall, make eye contact, and avoid crossing your arms or displaying defensive gestures. Project an open and welcoming demeanor to make the audience feel at ease.

Use Gestures and Movement: Incorporate purposeful gestures and movement to enhance engagement. Employ hand gestures to emphasize key points, and move around the stage to maintain audience interest. However, avoid excessive pacing, which can be distracting.

Control the Pace: Be mindful of the pace of your speech to keep the audience engaged. Speak at a comfortable and clear pace, allowing attendees to process the information. Avoid rushing through slides or content, as this can lead to disconnection and reduced comprehension.

Manage Your Time and Transitions: Ensure that your visuals transition smoothly and do not disrupt the flow of your presentation. Practice your speech with the visuals to ensure the timing aligns seamlessly with your narrative. A well-timed transition between slides keeps your audience focused and prevents distractions.

Visual aids are valuable tools in an estate planning presentation, but their impact lies in their thoughtful and strategic use. By focusing on impactful images, concise bullet points, and limited text, you can reinforce key points without overwhelming your audience. With a balanced approach to visual aids and a compelling delivery, you can create an immersive and informative estate planning experience for your audience.

Make It Clever

Well-timed humor can keep the energy moving in a presentation, especially if it's going to be a long one. Don't be afraid to toss in a groan-worthy dad joke or two, and you can't go wrong with a little self-deprecating humor. Here's how you can keep your seminar light and engaging:

> You can't go wrong with a little self-deprecating humor.

> *Use Your Wit:* Injecting wit and cleverness into your speech can captivate your audience's attention and leave a lasting impression. Humor can be a potent weapon in the arsenal of a skilled presenter, especially when tackling complex topics like estate planning. Injecting well-timed jokes and playful analogies not only captivates your audience but also makes intimidating concepts more approachable and relatable. To take your humor game to the next level, incorporating other media, such as images, videos, or memes, can add an extra layer of entertainment and keep your audience engaged throughout your presentation.

> *The Power of Laughter:* Laughter is a universal language that instantly breaks down barriers and

fosters a positive atmosphere in any setting. By interweaving humor into your estate planning speech, you create a relaxed and enjoyable environment, making your audience more receptive to your message. When your audience laughs, they experience a boost of dopamine, a feel-good neurotransmitter, which reinforces the pleasure of listening to your speech. This positive association ensures that your message leaves a lasting impression.

Relatability and Connection: Using humor allows you to connect with your audience on a personal level, showing them that you understand their concerns and are approachable. Crafting jokes that resonate with common experiences related to estate planning, such as will-writing procrastination or family squabbles over inheritance, establishes a shared connection and draws your listeners in to your presentation.

Visual Humor: While jokes and wordplay are effective, don't underestimate the power of visual humor to complement your speech. Incorporating amusing images, videos, or memes related to estate planning can create moments of delight for your audience. Visual humor serves as a visual aid that reinforces your points and adds a layer of entertainment to your presentation.

Engaging Your Audience: A lively, humorous presentation is more likely to hold your audience's attention throughout your speech. A monotonous, information-heavy presentation can lead to audience disengagement. By infusing humor and interactive elements into your speech, you keep your listeners attentive and create a memorable experience for them.

Cultural References: Humor based on pop culture or current events can resonate with diverse audiences and transcend generational gaps. Including relevant cultural references in your jokes and analogies ensures that your speech feels fresh and relatable to a broad range of listeners. It also showcases your awareness of current trends and adds an au courant touch to your presentation.

Strategic humor is a powerful tool that elevates an estate planning speech from mundane to memorable. By incorporating well-timed jokes, playful analogies, and clever visual humor, you create an engaging and enjoyable experience for your audience.

> Strategic humor is a powerful tool.

Humor fosters an atmosphere of relatability and connection, breaking down complex estate planning concepts into accessible ideas. As your audience laughs and connects with your message, they become more invested in your expertise and are more likely to take proactive steps toward securing their financial future.

MAKE IT PERSONABLE

You're the one in front of the room, so you're the one who needs to set the tone for the gathering. Being affable, personable, and open will help build trust with your audience. Consider these points to ensure that you're putting your best foot forward.

Be Authentic and Relatable: Share personal anecdotes and experiences to create a genuine connection. Relate to the audience by sharing relevant stories that illustrate the importance of estate planning. Authenticity fosters trust and makes the presentation more relatable.

Adapt to Audience Reactions: Be responsive to the audience's feedback and adjust your presentation accordingly. Pay attention to their facial expressions and body language. If you notice signs of confusion or disinterest, be prepared to clarify or redirect the discussion to re-engage the audience.

Handle Questions Confidently: Encourage questions and answer them confidently and concisely. Welcome audience inquiries and respond with clarity and expertise. If a question requires a more in-depth explanation, offer to discuss it further after the presentation.

Acknowledge Common Concerns: At the beginning of the presentation, address common doubts or skepticism attendees may have. Recognize that estate planning decisions can be overwhelming and that attendees may wonder about the potential sales pitch. Assure them that your intention is to provide valuable information and guidance, regardless of their decision to engage your services.

Establish Common Ground: Find areas of agreement with the audience to build rapport. Share anecdotes or insights that demonstrate your understanding of their perspectives. Relating to their experiences and concerns helps create a sense of connection and trust.

Share Success Stories: Incorporate success stories of past clients who were initially skeptical but ultimately benefited from proper estate planning. By highlighting real-life examples of individuals who were initially hesitant but found peace of mind and security through the process, you instill confidence in the value of estate planning.

Invite Questions and Feedback: Encourage the audience to share or write down their questions during the presentation. Any questions left unaddressed by the end of the presentation can be asked and answered in a subsequent strategy session. This open invitation fosters a sense of inclusion and makes the audience feel valued.

Provide Clear Explanations: Offer clear explanations of the estate planning process and its benefits. Address any misconceptions and provide transparent insights into the steps involved in estate planning. This helps dispel skepticism and empowers attendees to make informed decisions.

Demonstrate Expertise: Exude confidence and demonstrate your expertise in estate planning. A knowledgeable and self-assured presentation reinforces your credibility and competence, alleviating doubts about the value of the information being presented.

Offer Value Regardless of Engagement: Reiterate that attendees will gain valuable knowledge and insights from the seminar, regardless of their decision to proceed with your services. Emphasize that the goal is to provide educational content that equips them to make informed decisions, even if they choose to explore other avenues for estate planning.

Investing time in honing presentation skills can significantly elevate the impact of an estate planning seminar. A confident and captivating presenter commands attention and instills trust, leaving attendees with a memorable and empowering experience. As a result, honing these skills not only benefits the quality of the seminar but also strengthens your reputation as a knowledgeable and approachable estate planning professional.

Make It Entertaining

In the last chapter, we touched briefly on ways to keep boredom from creeping into your audience. Here are some tips and ideas you can try to keep your attendees actively engaged in your seminar:

Introduce Compelling Videos: Include short videos that illustrate real-life scenarios or showcase the impact of estate planning. A video testimonial from a client who experienced the benefits of proper estate planning can add a human touch to your presentation.

Alternatively, an animated video explaining the estate planning process step by step can make the content more accessible and visually appealing.

Offer Interactive Quizzes or Polls: Incorporate interactive quizzes or polls to involve your audience actively in the presentation. Ask thought-provoking questions related to estate planning or quiz your audience on common misconceptions. This encourages participation, stimulates critical thinking, and reinforces important concepts.

Use Audio Clips: Audio clips can be effective in delivering powerful narratives or testimonials. Play recorded interviews with experts, clients, or beneficiaries to provide additional insights or personal experiences. The emotional impact of hearing firsthand accounts can create a lasting impression on your audience.

Incorporate Interactive Decision-Making Exercises: Engage your audience with interactive exercises that prompt them to make hypothetical estate planning decisions. Present a case study and encourage your audience to discuss the best course of action. This activity not only facilitates active learning but also encourages open dialogue and peer-to-peer learning.

Visualize Data and Statistics: Use multimedia to present data and statistics in visually appealing formats. Infographics, charts, and graphs can help convey complex information in a concise and easily understandable manner. Visualizing data makes it more digestible and compelling for your audience.

Break Up Monotony: Introduce multimedia elements strategically to break up lengthy segments of talking. Incorporating short videos, audio clips, or interactive exercises at intervals keeps your audience engaged and prevents information overload. This variation maintains the energy and attentiveness of your listeners throughout the presentation.

Reinforce Key Points: Use multimedia to reinforce crucial messages and ensure they stick with your audience. Create a video summary at the end of each section, highlighting the main takeaways from the content covered. This recap solidifies understanding and underscores the importance of estate planning decisions.

Start with the Basics: Begin your presentation by laying a solid foundation of fundamental estate planning principles. Introduce key concepts such as wills, trusts, and powers of attorney in clear and concise terms. This provides a framework upon which to build more advanced ideas later in your speech.

Integrating multimedia elements into your estate planning presentation takes your communication to the next level. With multimedia, you can transform a traditional presentation into an interactive journey that keeps your listeners attentive, interested, and empowered to take proactive steps in their estate planning journey. As a result, your audience is

> Integrating multimedia elements into your estate planning presentation takes your communication to the next level.

more likely to retain the information, apply it to their unique situations, and embrace estate planning as a crucial means of protecting their assets and securing their loved ones' financial future.

MAKE IT EASY

When presenting an estate planning speech, it's crucial to provide your audience with clear, actionable steps that they can implement right away. Avoid using jargon or technical language that might confuse or intimidate listeners. Your goal is to empower them with practical advice and guidance, ensuring they feel confident in taking the necessary actions to protect their assets and loved ones. Here's how you can achieve this:

> *Simplify Complex Concepts*: Break down estate planning concepts into simple terms that anyone can understand. Rather than overwhelming your audience with legal jargon, use relatable language to explain the importance of wills, trusts, and powers of attorney. Clarify the significance of each element in protecting their assets and ensuring their wishes are honored.

> *Focus on Key Action Steps*: Provide a concise list of actionable steps that listeners can take immediately. For instance, encourage your audience to start by creating a basic will or setting up a living trust. Emphasize the importance of naming beneficiaries on retirement accounts and life insurance policies. By focusing on these vital actions, you inspire your audience to take tangible steps toward securing their financial future.

Offer DIY Strategies and Professional Guidance: Provide a balanced approach by offering DIY strategies for those comfortable doing their own planning, while also highlighting the benefits of seeking professional advice. Share resources and tools for basic estate planning that individuals can access on their own. At the same time, stress the value of consulting with an estate planning attorney to address more complex situations and ensure their plans are legally sound.

Use Analogies and Real-Life Scenarios: Make your advice relatable by using analogies and real-life scenarios that illustrate the importance of estate planning. Compare estate planning to creating a safety net for loved ones or planning for life's uncertainties, like insuring a valuable possession. Relatable comparisons like these help your audience grasp the tangible benefits of estate planning.

Encourage Questions and Provide Answers: Invite audience members to ask questions and address any concerns they might have. By encouraging open dialogue, you create a safe space for your audience to seek clarification and share their specific situations. Be prepared to provide thoughtful answers and reassurance, ensuring they feel supported in their estate planning journey.

Offer Follow-Up Resources: Provide handouts or links to additional information and resources for those who want to delve deeper into specific topics. Offer a one-page summary of the key action steps covered in your speech, along with links to reputable websites or informative articles. This way, your audience can continue their learning and decision-making process after the presentation.

In an estate planning speech, your primary objective is to empower your audience with actionable steps and guidance. By simplifying complex concepts, providing clear action items, and avoiding technical jargon, you make estate planning accessible and relatable. Through this approach, you inspire confidence and motivate individuals to take control of their financial legacies, ensuring their assets and loved ones are protected in the most effective way possible.

> Your primary objective is to empower your audience with actionable steps and guidance.

MAKE IT A CALL TO ACTION

Encouraging your audience to take concrete steps is a pivotal part of your estate planning presentation. A well-crafted call to action (CTA) can turn passive attendees into motivated individuals ready to take control of their financial future. By providing a compelling and exclusive incentive and attaching a deadline to it, you create a sense of urgency and inspire immediate action.

> Create a sense of urgency and inspire immediate action.

Emphasize the Exclusive Offer: Highlight the exceptional opportunity you're extending to your audience. Make it crystal clear that this offer is a privilege reserved solely for those at the presentation. Stress the inherent value they will gain from this offer, whether it's a complimentary consultation or an enlightening guide tailored to their needs.

Create a Sense of Urgency: Establish a specific deadline for the offer to spur immediate engagement. By introducing a time-sensitive CTA, you infuse a sense of urgency into your audience, motivating them to respond promptly. Convey that this time-bound offer is exclusively available to those who respond within the specified time frame.

Clearly Outline the Benefits: Articulate how the free consultation or informative guide will directly benefit your audience. Elaborate on the advantages they'll derive from the consultation, such as a personalized estate planning assessment or a comprehensive financial analysis. For the informative guide, emphasize the wealth of valuable insights and actionable tips it contains.

Provide Multiple Ways to Respond: Facilitate a seamless response process by offering your audience multiple contact options. Provide them with various channels to act upon the call to action, whether it's a contact number, an email address, or a website link to access the informative guide. The more accessible the response avenues, the higher the likelihood of prompt action.

Reiterate the Importance of Estate Planning: Reinforce the critical nature of safeguarding their assets and loved ones through proactive planning. Remind your audience that estate planning is a vital component of financial well-being for everyone, regardless of age or wealth. Stress how the consultation or informative guide will empower them to make informed decisions and secure their financial future.

Offer a Personal Touch: Convey your readiness to address any questions or concerns they may have. Assure your audience that you're available to provide personalized guidance and support. This personal commitment underscores your dedication to their best interests and fosters trust.

Encourage Immediate Action: Motivate your audience to act promptly and capitalize on this valuable opportunity. Employ persuasive language that emphasizes the consequences of delaying estate planning. Stress that by responding promptly, they can embark on the journey to safeguard their assets and secure their loved ones' futures without unnecessary delays.

A well-crafted call to action has the potential to transform passive attendees into proactive clients. Through a compelling and exclusive incentive, a well-defined deadline, and a focus on the benefits, you can ignite a sense of urgency that compels your audience to take immediate action. By encouraging action, you empower your audience to make informed decisions, ensuring their assets and loved ones are protected through effective estate planning strategies.

> A well-crafted call to action has the potential to transform passive attendees into proactive clients.

MAKE IT SCARY! (BUT NOT TOO MUCH!)

Enhance your presentation by sharing real-life horror stories resulting from inadequate estate planning. These personal cautionary tales, especially if they've affected you or your family, carry a profound impact, creating a strong emotional connection with your audience. By sharing these experiences, you underscore the crucial significance of proper estate planning, motivating your audience to act promptly to protect their assets and loved ones.

> Underscore the crucial significance of proper estate planning.

Highlight Consequences: Emphasize the potential repercussions of insufficient estate planning in these stories. Explain how the absence of a comprehensive plan can lead to family disputes, financial hardships, or delays in asset distribution. By vividly portraying these challenges and hardships, you stress the urgency of proactive planning to your audience.

Explain the Emotional Impact: Address the emotional toll that insufficient estate planning can inflict on surviving family members. Discuss how unresolved legal and financial matters can exacerbate grief and add stress during an already challenging time. By touching on the emotional aspects, you appeal to your audience's empathy and reinforce the importance of taking action to prevent such situations.

Connect to Solutions: Transition from the cautionary tales to practical solutions like drafting a will, setting up a trust, or appointing guardians for minor children.

Explain how these measures could have prevented the issues faced in the stories, offering peace of mind and protection for loved ones during difficult times.

Stress the Need for Action: After sharing these personal stories, encourage your audience not to delay estate planning. Emphasize that even a moment's hesitation can have significant consequences. Remind them that proper estate planning is an act of love and responsibility toward their family's well-being.

Prepare to address any concerns or hesitations your audience may have after sharing your personal stories. Provide reassurance to those who might be hesitant to start the planning process. Offering your expertise and support demonstrates your commitment to guiding them through the complexities of estate planning with care.

MAKE IT WORTH THEIR WHILE

Consider the benefits of partnering with a financial planning professional to enhance your presentation and broaden your services. By offering a complimentary bonus—a combined estate planning and financial planning consultation—you can provide substantial value to your audience while distinguishing yourself from competitors. To effectively integrate this into your presentation, include the following techniques:

Highlight the Collaboration: Emphasize how estate planning and financial planning work harmoniously to benefit your audience. Describe how this cooperation aligns their financial and estate goals, showcasing a holistic approach that addresses wealth accumulation, protection, and distribution.

Introduce the Bonus: Introduce the joint consultation as an exclusive and time-limited bonus for seminar attendees. Stress that it's available solely to those who attend your presentation and emphasize that this comprehensive consultation equips them to make informed decisions.

Pre-Frame the Benefits: Outline the specific advantages of the joint consultation, explaining how it helps create a unified financial plan aligned with estate goals. Highlight the holistic approach it provides to secure their financial future efficiently.

Consider a Special Rate: Consider offering a discounted rate for attendees who opt for the joint consultation. This reduced fee acts as an extra incentive, motivating attendees to act promptly and reinforcing the limited-time, exclusive nature of the offer.

Collaborate Effectively: Partner with a reputable financial planner who shares the event's costs. This collaborative effort not only eases the financial burden but also enhances the credibility of both professionals, instilling confidence in the comprehensive expertise provided.

Demonstrate the Value: Highlight the total value of the joint consultation, showcasing the significant benefit of the free bonus. Illustrate the monetary value of estate planning and financial planning services if acquired separately, underscoring the exceptional value offered.

Encourage Immediate Action: Urge attendees to seize the opportunity and schedule their consultation without delay. Remind them that financial circumstances can change quickly and waiting can have adverse consequences. Encourage them to take immediate action to secure their financial future through this exclusive offering.

By integrating a joint estate planning and financial planning consultation as a complimentary bonus, you provide your audience with a compelling incentive to advance in their financial journey. With a comprehensive package, you establish yourself as a trusted adviser, delivering outstanding value and fostering trust and security with your audience.

Make It Time for the Next Chapter

We've journeyed through a comprehensive guide on delivering impactful estate planning speeches, uncovering the strategies and techniques that can elevate your message from mundane to memorable. Personalization has been a recurring theme, and rightfully so. Tailoring your presentation to your strengths and personality as well as your audience's needs and concerns is the foundation upon which everything else is built. Sharing relatable stories from your own experiences or weaving in anecdotes that resonate with your listeners creates an emotional connection that transcends the impersonal nature of estate planning.

Visual appeal and interactivity also play pivotal roles in holding your audience's attention. In an era dominated by screens and instant gratification, incorporating multimedia elements such as videos, interactive exercises, and visually appealing slides adds dynamism and depth to your presentation. These tools are more than just attention grabbers; they are powerful aids for comprehension and retention.

Acknowledging and addressing your audience's initial doubts and concerns with empathy and authenticity can dissolve barriers and establish trust. Sharing cautionary tales of estate planning gone wrong reinforces the necessity of taking action and, in doing so, deepens your audience's connection to the topic.

Don't forget to use the call to action as the bridge between inspiration and action. By offering a valuable, time-limited incentive like a free consultation, you galvanize your audience to take the next steps in securing their financial future. The urgency you create and the personal touch you offer reinforce your commitment to their well-being.

> Don't forget to use the call to action as the bridge between inspiration and action.

Finally, considering a partnership with a financial planning professional brings comprehensive value to your presentation. The collaboration between estate planning and financial planning highlights the holistic approach your audience can benefit from, and offering a special rate for joint consultations is an enticing proposition.

Creating a compelling estate planning presentation is an art that blends personalization, visual engagement, empathy, and strategic collaboration. Each element plays a crucial role in inspiring your audience to take proactive steps in safeguarding their assets and loved ones. Ultimately, a well-structured and thoughtfully delivered estate planning speech doesn't just impart information; it instills confidence, motivates action, and builds lasting relationships with your audience.

CONCLUSION

TAKE THE PLUNGE

Changing practice areas can be scary, but estate planning really does offer a lucrative, time-friendly, low-stress alternative to traditional legal practice. Back in Chapter 4, I talked a lot about what's "wrong" with traditional practice and what's "right" about estate planning. In this last chapter, I want to go a little deeper into the things that make this area of practice exceptional to show you, once and for all, why you should take the plunge today.

First, Let's Talk About Money

We'll get this out of the way first because, honestly, money is great, but I don't want to make it all about the payout. That being said, most of us had expectations of making a comfortable salary when we became attorneys, right? Although law school can be

> Money is great, but I don't want to make it all about the payout.

hell, the silver lining on the other side of the bar exam is a stable career path, no matter what practice area we choose. So let's just be honest with ourselves about that.

Okay, so estate planning. Do it right (aka, the way I told you in Chapter 4!), and you will have a lucrative practice. Lawyers who deal with estate planning often work with clients possessing substantial assets and intricate family structures. These clients typically require highly customized and comprehensive estate plans, resulting in increased billable hours and revenue opportunities for attorneys.

You can charge competitive fees for your expertise in estate planning. Given the complexity and high value of estate planning services, you can also command higher fees compared to more routine legal matters. Clients are often willing to pay for the expertise and assurance that their estate plans are comprehensive and well crafted.

The Stress Reduction Is Priceless

Estate planning is an excellent choice for lawyers who value a balanced work-life routine. This area of law offers a time-friendly legal practice that promotes a healthier work-life balance compared to many other legal fields. Let's explore how the time-friendly nature of estate planning can contribute to a more fulfilling professional and personal life for you.

Consistent Work Hours: In estate planning, you'll deal with fewer urgent and time-sensitive matters, which translates to more consistent work hours. Unlike litigators, who often face unexpected emergencies and last-minute hearings, estate planning attorneys can plan their workload in advance. This means you can better manage your time and reduce the chances of disruptive schedule changes.

Advance Planning Opportunities: Estate planning attorneys have the luxury of proactively scheduling client consultations and planning their tasks in advance. Estate planning services typically involve consultations with clients to assess their needs and goals. You can schedule these meetings well ahead of time, allowing for efficient time allocation and minimal disruptions to your other work commitments.

Fewer Court Appearances: As an estate planning attorney, you'll have fewer court appearances, leading to a more predictable schedule. While litigators spend considerable time in courtrooms, you'll typically attend fewer hearings. This means fewer interruptions to your daily tasks and more focus on crafting comprehensive estate plans.

Longer-Term Projects: Estate planning cases generally have longer timelines, which allows for better planning and organization. Unlike litigation cases that may require immediate attention and quick turnarounds, estate planning projects unfold over weeks or months. This longer time frame lets you allocate your time efficiently and prioritize tasks based on client needs and deadlines.

Flexibility for Work-Life Integration: Estate planning's predictable schedule enables you to integrate your work and personal life more effectively. You can better plan your days, making it easier to manage personal commitments alongside your professional responsibilities. This flexibility contributes to a healthier work-life balance and improved overall well-being.

> This flexibility contributes to a healthier work-life balance.

Reduced Stress Levels: With fewer time constraints and urgent deadlines, estate planning attorneys often experience lower stress levels. A more predictable workload and a reduced sense of urgency in estate planning contribute to a less stressful work environment. This, in turn, supports better decision-making and fosters a positive outlook on your legal career.

Estate planning offers you the opportunity to have a fulfilling legal career while enjoying a well-balanced personal life. The time-friendly aspects of estate planning, including consistent work hours, advance planning opportunities, fewer court appearances, longer-term projects, flexibility for work-life integration, and reduced stress levels, make it an attractive choice for attorneys seeking a balanced and rewarding legal practice.

Some "Work Perks" of the Practice

There are some things about estate planning that I really love, and they just sort of come along with the nature of the job. It's such a client-focused specialty, which means building great relationships and much more. This approach empowers clients by providing comprehensive plans to protect their wealth and legacy. By engaging in thoughtful conversations, you gain insights into their unique circumstances, family dynamics, and financial objectives. In this way, you can ensure that each estate plan is tailored to the individual client's situation, fostering trust and satisfaction.

Estate planning encourages long-term relationships with clients and their families. The ongoing nature of estate planning creates lasting client relationships that are built on trust, care, and dedication. By providing peace of mind and addressing clients' evolving needs, estate planning attorneys play a vital role in securing their clients' financial future and their loved ones' well-being. This ongoing process of collaboration fosters a rewarding and enduring relationship, ensuring that clients view their estate planning attorneys as trusted advisers throughout their lives.

Estate plans must be flexible to accommodate life changes like marriages, births, deaths, and financial fluctuations. Estate planning attorneys guide clients through these significant life events, ensuring that estate plans reflect their current wishes and circumstances. This ongoing support builds trust and confidence in the attorney's expertise. Plus, estate planning attorneys stay informed about evolving estate planning laws and regulations to keep clients' plans compliant and optimized.

Legal frameworks related to estate planning can change over time, and attorneys must remain up-to-date. Regular reviews of estate plans allow attorneys to proactively address any legal modifications that may impact clients' plans. Incorporating flexibility into estate plans and staying ahead of legal changes are essential aspects of estate planning that benefit clients and ensure the ongoing effectiveness of their plans.

That means that clients feel reassured and confident in their estate plans, knowing that they have taken proactive measures to protect their loved ones. The consultative approach instills a sense of security in clients, who know that their assets are safeguarded and their wishes are documented. This sense of security strengthens the client-lawyer relationship and leads to client satisfaction.

This reassurance is especially important for families with young children. Many families with minor children are unaware of the importance of estate planning in securing their children's future. Estate planning attorneys can actively educate and engage families with minor children about the necessity of guardianship designations and trust arrangements. By crafting estate plans that protect

> Many families with minor children are unaware of the importance of estate planning in securing their children's future.

children from the foster-care system and ensure they are cared for by designated guardians, you fill a significant need in the market.

High-net-worth individuals require sophisticated estate planning strategies to preserve and grow their wealth. Estate planning attorneys can tailor their services to address the complex financial portfolios of affluent clients. By providing advanced estate planning techniques like tax planning, irrevocable trusts, and wealth preservation strategies, you can attract high-net-worth individuals seeking this type of curated advice.

Serving high-net-worth individuals also often means helping them seek opportunities to engage in philanthropy and charitable giving. Estate planning attorneys can collaborate with charitable organizations to help clients incorporate charitable giving into their estate plans. If you can offer guidance on creating charitable trusts, donor-advised funds, or planned giving strategies, you can also facilitate clients' altruistic goals while maximizing tax benefits.

The recurring theme here is client relationships. If you can stay laser-focused on being a client-driven practice that offers tailored solutions for each estate plan, you'll be well on your way to building an incredible clientele and an incredible reputation. When you can serve your clients' needs with care, expertise, and complete services, your practice will become the ultimate total package for estate planning.

Stay Ahead of the Curve

The future is now, folks. Let's talk about why you need to hop into estate planning as soon as possible. The field of estate planning is currently experiencing significant growth due to several key factors:

Baby Boomers: The aging population is a major driver, as the baby boomer generation, born between 1946 and 1964, is now reaching retirement age. This generation comprises a substantial portion of the population and is actively planning for their retirement and beyond. As baby boomers age, estate planning becomes a critical consideration, and lawyers focusing on this field are well positioned to address their unique needs and concerns. This presents you with a substantial and growing client base among the aging population.

Awareness: There is a rising awareness of the importance of estate planning among individuals and families. People are becoming more informed about the consequences of not having a proper estate plan in place. They are increasingly aware of the potential risks and challenges that can arise without a comprehensive estate plan. This heightened awareness is driving more individuals to seek professional assistance in safeguarding their assets, ensuring the smooth transfer of wealth, and making informed decisions about their health care and end-of-life preferences. Estate planning attorneys can capitalize on this growing awareness by offering comprehensive solutions tailored to each client's unique needs and circumstances.

> Estate planning attorneys can capitalize on this growing awareness.

Evolving Family Structures: Evolving family structures are creating a demand for estate planning strategies. Modern families often have complex dynamics, such as blended families, multigenerational households, and same-sex partnerships. These changing family structures require more sophisticated estate planning approaches to address the complexities of inheritance, guardianship, and asset distribution. Lawyers with expertise in estate planning can provide customized solutions that accommodate these diverse family arrangements, making their services indispensable in the evolving legal landscape.

Transfer of Wealth: Sharing wealth from one generation to the next creates a need for legal advice to preserve assets and minimize tax implications. As baby boomers pass on their wealth to their heirs, individuals and families are seeking guidance on how to preserve family legacies and optimize their financial planning. Estate planning attorneys can provide invaluable assistance in minimizing estate taxes and maximizing the assets passed down to beneficiaries, thereby playing a pivotal role in securing their clients' financial future.

Business Legacies: Business owners often have unique estate planning needs, such as succession planning and asset protection. Estate planning attorneys can offer comprehensive solutions that address the complexities of transferring ownership and management of businesses to the next generation. By assisting business owners in creating succession plans and safeguarding their business assets, attorneys become valuable partners in securing their clients' legacies.

Peace of Mind in an Uncertain World: Finally, estate planning offers clients peace of mind about the future. In today's complex world, financial planning can create uncertainty and stress. Clients appreciate the reassurance that comes with knowing their affairs are in order, their assets are protected, and their wishes are documented. This sense of security strengthens the bond between clients and their estate planning attorneys, leading to higher levels of client satisfaction and loyalty.

Lawyers who recognize and adapt to these demographic shifts are well positioned to thrive in this evolving legal landscape by serving a diverse and expanding client base. By extending their expertise to include the aging boomer population, business owners, charitable organizations, high-net-worth individuals, and families with minor children, attorneys can tap into new areas of demand and broaden the scope of their legal services.

There's one last thing we need to discuss before we wrap up: death. Assisting clients with estate administration after a loved one's passing is a natural extension of estate planning services. Estate planning attorneys can offer compassionate guidance and support to families during the estate settlement process. By helping executors navigate legal procedures, probate, and asset distribution, attorneys extend their services beyond estate planning, reinforcing their role as trusted advisers throughout various life stages.

THIS IS THE END (ALMOST)

Revamping your practice area as an estate planning attorney opens up exciting possibilities. It not only allows you to serve a diverse range of clients but also positions you as a sought-after adviser across a broad spectrum of legal matters. The rising demand for estate planning services, particularly for families with minor children, emphasizes the crucial role you play in securing the future of vulnerable dependents. By offering a comprehensive suite of estate planning solutions, you strengthen your position as a trusted adviser and leave a lasting positive impact on the lives of your clients and their loved ones.

Estate planning provides a path to a lucrative, time-friendly, and low-stress alternative to traditional legal practice. The potential for higher earnings, greater work-hour flexibility, and reduced stress levels makes estate planning an attractive choice for a fulfilling and rewarding legal career. Plus, you have the chance to profoundly influence your clients' lives, cultivate long-term relationships, and serve a growing demographic, which further enhances the appeal of estate planning as your practice area. As the demand for estate planning services continues to rise, you can carve out a successful and satisfying niche within the legal profession.

In addition to these advantages, you can offer flat-fee value billing, providing yourself with financial freedom and flexibility in delivering legal services. Embracing technology and innovative tools becomes paramount in this evolving legal landscape, enabling you to streamline your workflow and enhance client engagement. By placing your clients' needs at the forefront and maintaining clear communication, you can forge stronger relationships and offer personalized services, ensuring your thriving presence in the dynamic field of estate planning. So seize the opportunity and embark on this exciting journey to expand your practice and shape a brighter future for your clients and yourself.

> Embracing technology and innovative tools becomes paramount.

And so we (sort of) come to the end of our journey together. This is the last regular chapter of the book, but there's still much more I want to share with you, so please enjoy the two bonus chapters you'll find after this one. Thanks for coming along on this journey, and I hope you'll thoroughly consider changing your practice area to estate planning. I couldn't have done more to try and convince you...

Oh, wait; yes, I could have—go check out the bonus chapters!

BONUS CHAPTER 1

WORKING WITH A FINANCIAL PLANNER

Hey, welcome to the first bonus chapter! Here, we're going to discuss the benefits of collaborating with a financial planner to offer clients a more comprehensive estate planning experience. Here's why, in a nutshell, this is a good idea:

- *Legal Aspects*: Estate planning lawyers have in-depth knowledge of probate laws, tax implications related to inheritance, and legal structures like trusts and estates. They ensure that a client's wishes are documented properly and are in compliance with the law.
- *Financial Strategy*: Financial planners, on the other hand, are trained to assess and strategize around a client's entire financial picture. They can advise on how assets should be distributed, taking into consideration

potential tax implications, growth opportunities, and the financial well-being of the heirs.

Let's take a closer look.

Benefits for Clients

Collaboration between estate planning lawyers and financial planners brings clients a wealth of benefits, ensuring that the legal and financial aspects of estate planning are handled with precision. Here, we'll examine the advantages of this partnership, including streamlined processes, enhanced client trust, proactive adjustments, and greater client satisfaction. By combining their expertise, these professionals create a holistic approach to estate planning that empowers clients to make informed decisions about their financial future and the legacy they leave behind.

> Collaboration between estate planning lawyers and financial planners brings clients a wealth of benefits.

Financial planners have an intricate understanding of their client's financial landscape, encompassing assets, liabilities, investments, and insurance. This detailed knowledge becomes a valuable asset when collaborating with estate planning lawyers. Upon the client's approval, financial planners can seamlessly share this meticulously organized financial data with lawyers. This collaborative effort significantly streamlines the estate planning process, saving lawyers valuable time that would otherwise be spent collecting and organizing financial information. Consequently, this accelerates the estate planning process and ensures that each financial decision is rooted in a comprehensive understanding of the client's financial world.

Clients referred to estate planning lawyers by trusted financial planners bring a pre-established level of trust and a foundational grasp of estate planning concepts. The endorsement from a financial adviser fosters trust and paves the way for a smoother initial client-lawyer relationship. Thanks to their financial planner's guidance, these clients often enter the process with a solid understanding of estate planning. Lawyers can thus focus on building upon the client's existing knowledge, making the process more collaborative and efficient.

Financial planners engage in periodic financial reviews with their clients—a practice that serves as a reminder to revisit estate plans. These professionals are well equipped to detect significant changes in their client's financial situation and can recommend timely estate plan reviews. As life transitions unfold, financial planners are often the first to notice discrepancies or opportunities that impact the client's estate plan. These insights, stemming from a profound understanding of the client's financial landscape, prompt proactive adjustments to ensure estate plans remain relevant and aligned with the client's evolving financial story.

The collaborative efforts of lawyers and financial planners provide clients with a sense that all aspects of their estate, both legal and financial, are handled with expertise and care. This comprehensive approach enhances client satisfaction and fosters long-term loyalty. Collaboration between estate planning lawyers and financial planners optimizes the estate planning process, enhances trust, facilitates timely updates, and ultimately ensures clients' peace of mind and satisfaction. By combining legal and financial expertise, this collaborative approach empowers clients to make informed decisions about their assets and financial future while safeguarding their legacy.

Benefits for the Professionals

Collaboration extends beyond client services. Joint marketing efforts, seminars, and event organization allow estate planning lawyers and financial planners to share expenses, resulting in higher-quality outreach materials and events while reducing individual costs. This cost-sharing dynamic enhances the overall quality of their outreach endeavors and lightens the financial burden on each professional.

With each professional bringing their own client base and network to the table, collaborative events enable them to tap into the other's audience, effectively broadening their reach and acquiring new clients. This symbiotic sharing of audiences strengthens their collective expertise, facilitating an efficient exchange of knowledge and referrals. Plus, collaboration between professionals from different fields enhances the credibility of the information shared during joint endeavors. This collaboration conveys a well-rounded perspective that considers various facets of estate and financial planning, reassuring audiences of the depth and comprehensiveness of the insights provided. This increased credibility is invaluable in a world where discerning audiences seek well-rounded knowledge.

> Collaboration conveys a well-rounded perspective.

For estate planning lawyers hosting seminars with financial planners as speakers, this collaboration offers clients a fresh perspective on estate planning intricacies directly from a legal expert and a finance expert, enriching their understanding and making the seminar more valuable. This fresh perspective reinvigorates the client experience and fosters ongoing learning. Alternating roles in seminars, where one professional becomes the speaker while the other listens, facilitates mutual growth. Insights from one field enhance the understanding and service offerings of the other, ensuring both remain abreast of developments in both sectors. This continuous learning process is enriching for professionals and beneficial for clients.

Collaboration leads to symbiotic referrals as clients identify their specific needs through post-seminar reflection. Clients are directed to the professional most suited to address their immediate requirements, ensuring prequalified client engagement. This not only benefits clients but also strengthens the collaborative relationship.

Joint marketing and seminars present a unified brand message, simplifying the audience's experience. This approach creates a powerful narrative encompassing the combined strength and expertise of both fields, making it easier for potential clients to recall and seek their services when needed. It forms a memorable and cohesive presence in the market. Using digital platforms such as websites, social-media channels, and email lists for collaborative promotion amplifies outreach efforts. This approach engages diverse audience segments, reaching those interested in financial planning or estate law through each professional's digital footprint. It maximizes online visibility and engagement.

Collaborative planning streamlines the logistical aspects of seminars, from venue selection and event promotion to material preparation and post-seminar follow-ups. By dividing responsibilities based on expertise, professionals ensure a more efficiently planned and executed event, ultimately benefiting both the audience and themselves. Successful seminars can evolve into long-term partnerships. Regular annual or biannual seminars, joint workshops, or online webinars promise consistent value delivery to their shared audience, reinforcing brand presence and updating clients on the latest developments. This ongoing collaboration ensures that both professionals continue to offer relevant and updated services.

A collaborative relationship between estate planning lawyers and financial planners exemplifies the power of professional partnerships. It streamlines workflows, elevates client satisfaction, and deepens the understanding of estate planning intricacies. This collaborative approach creates a landscape where mutual benefits extend far beyond client services, offering professionals opportunities for growth, networking, and brand enhancement. In a world where complexities in finance and estate law intertwine, the collaboration between these experts is not just a partnership; it's a journey toward creating a more secure and informed future for their clients. Together, they navigate the intricate web of legal and financial considerations, ensuring that each client's tapestry of wealth and security is woven with precision, care, and expertise.

> This collaborative approach creates a landscape where mutual benefits extend far beyond client services.

More Bonuses Ahead!

The collaborative landscape we've explored isn't just about enhancing practices; it's about building a more secure and informed future for clients. It's a reminder that in the world of finance and law, knowledge is indeed power, and combining that power through collaboration unlocks a multitude of possibilities. As estate planning lawyers and financial planners continue to evolve in this dynamic landscape, their partnership serves as a beacon, guiding clients toward a wealthier and more secure tomorrow, one collaborative step at a time.

I've got one more chapter for you before we end the book for good, so I hope you'll join me for one more go-around as we talk about collaborating with yet another professional—the professional speaker.

BONUS CHAPTER 2

WORKING WITH A PROFESSIONAL SPEAKER

Hey, folks. Here's the last chapter, and I'm so grateful you stuck with me for so long. Before we end the book, I want to add one more thing to the conversation about seminars: the potential of hiring a professional speaker to deliver your content instead of doing it yourself. There are a few reasons you might consider doing this, not the least of which is that stage fright is a real thing. Or perhaps you've got a bead on a particularly popular speaker who could draw in a big audience. Whatever your reasoning, let's examine why working with a professional speaker might work for you.

Clear Content Delivery

In many industries, including law, there's often a significant gap between specialized knowledge and what the general public understands. This gap doesn't reflect a lack of intelligence on the audience's part but is due to the complex language, intricate structures, and sometimes puzzling principles that define legal discussions. Skilled presenters serve as bridges, helping to connect abstract and complex legal concepts with tangible and understandable explanations.

> Skilled presenters serve as bridges.

Being able to simplify complex legal ideas isn't just about using plain language; it's about weaving a compelling narrative. Effective presenters don't just recite facts; they frame information, draw analogies, tell stories, and use visual aids to make concepts relatable and memorable. They anticipate questions, ensuring that the material not only makes sense at the moment but also remains clear afterward.

Estate planning provides a prime example of where this skill is invaluable. It's a field filled with legal complexities and emotional weight. For many, it's uncharted territory, laden with terms like "probate," "trusts," "executor," and "beneficiary." Beyond the jargon, it involves intricate decisions with implications and potential pitfalls. Presenters play a crucial role here. They must guide the audience through this complex terrain with empathy and precision, ensuring that the audience emerges with a clear understanding and appreciation of the subject's importance.

There are multiple benefits of this clarity for the audience. They can make informed decisions, feel more confident, and take action with purpose. This demystification empowers them, making a potentially intimidating topic manageable and actionable. In essence, while legal expertise involves understanding the intricacies of the law, presentation expertise ensures others can understand them too. In estate planning, where decisions can profoundly affect families and loved ones, this ability to bring clarity from complexity isn't just valuable—it's essential.

SAVE TIME AND BUILD CREDIBILITY

In the world of public speaking, professional presenters stand out, often due to their specialized training and extensive experience. Unlike the average person, these experts have honed their skills over numerous engagements, making them adept at capturing and retaining the audience's attention. They understand audience dynamics and can convey information in ways that resonate, ensuring that the core messages aren't just delivered but are also remembered. Beyond content delivery, they excel in interaction. When faced with questions, whether simple or challenging, they respond with ease and clarity. Essentially, the expertise of a professional presenter goes beyond merely speaking—it's about establishing a connection, ensuring understanding, and fostering an environment where knowledge flows seamlessly.

In legal practice, every minute counts. Crafting a seminar is a significant undertaking, from its inception to its delivery. It involves planning, research, scriptwriting, and rehearsal. The intricacies of assembling a coherent, informative, and engaging session require considerable effort and time—a luxury many lawyers may not have amidst their busy schedules.

> The intricacies of assembling a coherent, informative, and engaging session require considerable effort and time.

This is where professional presenters come in. With their expertise, they can swiftly navigate the seminar's planning and execution, freeing the lawyer from grappling with the ins and outs of public speaking or the technicalities of presentation software. With a professional speaker on the job, the lawyer can spend their time more productively. Instead of being bogged down by the details of seminar preparation, they can focus on their primary responsibilities. By entrusting the task of seminar presentation to a professional, the lawyer optimizes their time. They can maintain their commitment to clients and manage their practice effectively without being stretched thin.

Credibility is invaluable in the professional world, especially in fields where trust is paramount, such as legal practice. When a lawyer collaborates with a respected presenter known for excellence, it's not just a meeting of minds; it's a strategic alignment that can enhance the seminar's perceived value and authenticity.

Consider this: a respected professional brings not only their expertise but also their reputation. Their past accomplishments, proficiency in the subject, and ability to communicate effectively all serve as implicit endorsements. When they stand in front of an audience to present or introduce a lawyer, they lend some of their own credibility to the event. It's as if they're saying, "This content and this collaboration meet my standards."

This endorsement's ripple effect can extend beyond the seminar. The community, whether other professionals, potential clients, or the general public, may view the lawyer differently. The association with a distinguished presenter can bolster the lawyer's reputation, making them not just another legal expert but one endorsed by recognized authorities in related fields.

This collaboration acts as a seal of quality. It assures attendees that the content they're receiving has been vetted and deemed worthy by professionals they respect. As a result, the lawyer's standing in the community is not only maintained but potentially elevated, setting the stage for further opportunities and enhanced trust.

Knowing How to Connect

The effectiveness of any presentation often hinges on how well it resonates with the audience. Professionals specializing in seminar presentations understand and thoroughly use this fundamental principle, especially when potential clients are in attendance.

One of the hallmarks of an experienced presenter is the ability to tailor content to the audience's nuances. They recognize that a one-size-fits-all approach rarely works. Different audiences have varying needs, interests, and levels of prior knowledge. For instance, potential clients might be more interested in real-world applications, benefits, and outcomes of legal services rather than intricate legal jargon or theoretical discussions.

Tailoring presentations to this audience demographic means focusing on content directly relevant to their concerns and aspirations. A professional crafts the narrative to highlight the immediate benefits of the lawyer's services, shares relatable success stories, and provides actionable insights. This makes the presentation engaging and sets the stage for a more sales-conducive environment.

> A professional crafts the narrative to highlight the immediate benefits of the lawyer's services.

The art of tailoring doesn't end with content. Delivery style, choice of visual aids, anecdotes, and even pace can be adjusted to cater to the audience's preferences and expectations. Such meticulous customization ensures that the audience feels seen and understood, making them more receptive to the message.

Furthermore, by ensuring the material aligns with the audience's needs, a professional presenter indirectly prepares them for the sales process. When potential clients understand the value proposition and envision how the services meet their needs, they're more open to discussions, consultations, and engagements. A well-tailored presentation doesn't just educate; it lays the foundation for fruitful business relationships.

The key to a captivating presentation doesn't solely lie in content or visuals; it also rests in the presenter's ability to adjust dynamically based on real-time audience feedback. The room's energy, collective attentiveness, and even subtle shifts in body language provide crucial cues. A skilled presenter recognizes these signals and navigates the presentation in response to them.

Facial expressions are often the most immediate indicator of audience engagement. Furrowed brows may signal confusion, prompting the presenter to simplify or reiterate certain points. Nods, smiles, or attentive postures indicate agreement or interest, encouraging the presenter to delve deeper or proceed confidently.

Body language offers another layer of insight. Crossed arms might signify skepticism or disengagement, prompting the presenter to re-engage with questions, anecdotes, or lighthearted humor. Upright postures, note-taking, or focused gazes typically signify an engaged audience, indicating that the material is resonating with them.

However, it's not just about observing; it's about responding in real time. If a segment induces yawns or wandering eyes, a seasoned presenter might adjust the pace or skip to a more engaging section. Conversely, if there's intrigue or visible eagerness, it's wise to slow down, provide more detail, or invite immediate questions.

Tone and volume modulation also play vital roles. For instance, if the audience appears restless or distracted, a change in tone or volume can recapture their attention. A sudden shift from a soft-spoken narrative to a passionate proclamation can re-engage the audience.

Lastly, the ability to adjust doesn't mean constant pivoting. It's about achieving a delicate balance: adhering to the core message and structure of the presentation while being flexible enough to shift gears when needed.

A Fresh Perspective

Introducing an external presenter, especially one recognized as an authority in their field, can be transformative for both the audience and the lawyer hosting the seminar. This can be effective for several reasons.

Diverse perspectives can be a catalyst for innovation. An external expert, free from a particular law firm's internal processes, traditions, or biases, approaches topics differently. Their unique experiences, training, and interactions shape their perspective, allowing them to view issues from another angle.

This fresh outlook can lead to the discovery of overlooked nuances. What seems like a standard procedure or an accepted truth within a particular legal circle could be questioned, expanded upon, or even refuted by an external expert. They might highlight new research, reference international case studies, or draw parallels to other fields, enriching the understanding of familiar topics.

The introduction of new methodologies and strategies is another potential benefit. Legal practices evolve because of innovations in related fields or the exchange of ideas between different legal cultures. An external presenter can introduce novel techniques, tools, or strategies that have proven successful elsewhere but that you haven't considered yet.

> An external presenter can introduce novel techniques, tools, or strategies.

From the lawyer's perspective, this fresh input can be immensely valuable. It provides an opportunity for self-reflection and growth. Exposure to new perspectives allows lawyers to critically evaluate their practices, identifying areas for improvement or innovation. You might discover that certain strategies you've employed could be improved, or you might be inspired to dig deeper into areas of law or process that you previously considered peripheral.

Additionally, for the audience, whether peers or potential clients, including an authoritative external voice can be enlightening and reassuring. It signals the host lawyer's openness to learning and growth, fostering trust and demonstrating the lawyer's commitment to staying updated and versatile in their practice. The value of an external expert goes beyond knowledge transfer. They act as a mirror, reflecting strengths and gaps in existing practices, and as a window, offering glimpses into new horizons and possibilities in legal strategies and ideas.

SHOULD YOU OUTSOURCE?

Speaking in public is an art, but for many, it's intimidating. The thought of standing in front of an audience, with all eyes on the speaker, can evoke anxiety. For professionals like lawyers, whose strength lies in legal knowledge and argumentative skills, the added stress of public speaking can be overwhelming.

Outsourcing this task to a professional presenter can be a strategic move. It allows a more experienced and comfortable public speaker to take the lead, relieving the lawyer of the performance burden. This doesn't mean the lawyer is less involved; instead, it allows them to channel their energy and expertise into what they excel at. They can focus on building a robust case, researching relevant laws, and strategizing without worrying about stage or courtroom performance.

> This doesn't mean the lawyer is less involved.

Delegating the public-speaking aspect allows the lawyer to navigate around potential presentation pitfalls and stressors, ensuring their primary focus remains undiluted. They can dedicate themselves to the intricacies of their profession, confident that their message will be effectively delivered by someone skilled in public speaking.

Within the context of seminars, it's not just the speaker's knowledge or eloquence that matters; the ambiance, technical details, and interactive elements play crucial roles in making an impact. Engaging a professional for a seminar often brings dedicated teams and specialized tools. The tools a professional brings can significantly enhance the seminar's production value. Advanced sound equipment ensures clear and crisp audio without interference or echo. Visual tools can transform a presentation into a visual feast with dynamic slides, videos, or augmented-reality elements that captivate and educate simultaneously.

In an era where audience engagement is paramount, the interactive elements professionals incorporate can make all the difference. Live polls, quizzes, and interactive sessions foster participation and maintain audience attention. These elements make the seminar engaging and ensure that the information presented is understood and retained.

While seminar content is essential, the way it's presented plays a significant role in its success. By leveraging the expertise of a professional with their team and tools, you can ensure that a seminar isn't just informative but also memorable, engaging, and of the highest production quality. When it comes to professional presentations, some individuals carry more than just skills; they have cultivated loyal followings through years of dedication and consistent delivery. Their followers eagerly await their insights and recommendations. Therefore, collaborating with such professional presenters isn't just about partnering with a skilled individual; it's also about gaining exposure through their extensive networks. Their reach, amplified by their followers, is a significant force.

For lawyers, this collaboration opens up new possibilities. Suddenly, their message, expertise, and offerings become accessible to a different audience. This new audience, primarily followers of the presenter, could become future clients, collaborators, or advocates of the lawyer's services. The diversity of this newfound audience offers fresh perspectives and opportunities for professional growth.

Furthermore, the association with a renowned professional presenter adds credibility to the lawyer's profile. Being endorsed by someone with the trust and respect of a vast audience elevates the lawyer's standing in the eyes of this new crowd. This implicit endorsement serves as a strong foundation for the

> The association with a renowned professional presenter adds credibility to the lawyer's profile.

lawyer to engage with the audience and establish themselves as a trustworthy expert.

ONLY YOU CAN DECIDE

It's important to acknowledge the potential drawbacks of hiring a professional speaker. Some clients or audience members may prefer to hear directly from the lawyer for a more personal touch or to assess their expertise firsthand. It may also be out of your financial reach to pay expensive speaker's fees when you are just starting out running your seminars. You should always evaluate the pros and cons to determine if collaborating with a professional aligns with your goals and brand.

The role of professional speakers as bridge-builders, simplifiers of complex concepts, and dynamic communicators proves invaluable in enhancing clarity, credibility, and engagement. While exploring these benefits, it's essential to recognize the potential for fruitful collaborations with external experts and the profound impact of presentation excellence on your legal practice.

And with that, we've come to the end of our time together! If you haven't already done so, check out the conclusion, found just before these two bonus chapters, for parting pearls of wisdom and additional resources to help you lose the suit and build your practice.